A Journey From Anger to Peace

Be Angry but Do Not Sin

Patrick Coman

(with Chapter 8 by Veronica Coman)

A Journey From Anger to Peace
Copyright © 2023 by Patrick Coman

All rights reserved. No part of this publication may be reproduced, distributed, or transmitted in any form or by any means, including photocopying, recording, or other electronic or mechanical methods, without the prior written permission of the author, except in the case of brief quotations embodied in critical reviews and certain other non-commercial uses permitted by copyright law.

Tellwell Talent
www.tellwell.ca

ISBN
978-1-77941-375-8 (Hardcover)
978-1-77941-374-1 (Paperback)
978-1-77941-376-5 (eBook)

TABLE OF CONTENTS

Foreword vii
Preface ix
Acknowledgements xiii
Chapter 1:   My Journey 1
Chapter 2:   Anger 18
Chapter 3:   Responses to Anger 51
Chapter 4:   The Bible on Anger 58
Chapter 5:   I Don't Know Why I Get Angry 65
Chapter 6:   Anger and Demonisation 72
Chapter 7:   Dave's Story 74
Chapter 8:   Living with an Angry Person 76
Conclusion 83
References 87
Appendix 1: A Flow Chart of The Anger Cycle 89
Appendix 2: A Bible Study on Anger Triggers 91
Appendix 3: More Information on Demonisation 99
Appendix 4: Scriptures Used in This Book 107
Appendix 5: Receiving the Gift of Eternal Life 109

FOREWORD

It was pride that changed angels into devils; it is humility that makes men as angels.
Saint Augustine

Patrick Coman is an honest bloke who speaks from the heart, sharing his own journey of pain, brokenness, violence, and anger into self-awareness and self-respect. Patrick readily acknowledges his failings, and points to the grace of God in Jesus Christ that has over his lifetime brought him into a place of wholeness and peace.

I have known Patrick for over 40 years and journeyed with him, on and off, from the day he put his faith in Jesus Christ in his little farmhouse on the Darling Scarp near Pinjarra, WA.

His journey cannot be told without the presence of his wife, Veronica, who was the object of his rage at times, and yet in her own testimony of God's grace toward her, has remained with Patrick, and served beside him as faithful pastors and ministers of the Gospel of Jesus Christ—even while Patrick was still on a journey towards wholeness.

Of course, Patrick, like us all who follow Christ, is still on that journey to wholeness! He would say, along with the apostle Paul, "Not that I have already obtained all this, or have already arrived at my goal, but I press on to take hold of that for which Christ Jesus took hold of me" (Philippians 3:12, NIV,2011).

His testimony here is raw, honest, and undergirded by some of the powerful insights into the roots of anger and bitterness that he has learned along the way. And God has honoured the heart of Patrick to love and serve Jesus Christ—even when sometimes expressed in unhelpful ways in his early journey of faith. Patrick has always been passionate to introduce others to Jesus Christ as saviour because of his own experience of the transforming grace of God in Christ. And this passion continues to motivate him today in his senior years.

Others might not struggle with anger to the same degree as Patrick, but all can benefit from self-examination and application of principles outlined here. And most of all we can encounter the living Jesus Christ as Patrick has done. I commend this heartfelt book to all who desire to grow in grace and more and more into the likeness of the character of Jesus Christ.

Dr Kenn Iskov
Pastor & Theological Educator

PREFACE

In writing this book, I have shared very personal information that brought me great shame and caused my wife and her family distress and pain. Circumstances in my life have caused me to become a very angry and damaged person who then perpetrated some terrible acts. Forgiveness has set me free. Despite this, every time I see a scene of domestic violence on TV, I feel pain and regret for the times I inflicted this distress upon my wife and her family. We have talked about it and—although she assures me it is in the past and I am totally forgiven—I still have a very raw spot that domestic violence triggers, and I feel remorseful. In his 1981 book *Anger: Yours, Mine and What To Do About It*, R. P. Walters states there are two forces that can cause anger: external and internal. He goes on to say, external forces are conditions in our physical and social environment such as: a loss, a threat, frustration, or rejection. When these occur, even if a person appears to be coping, it is quite probable they are feeling angry due to these external forces. When people become angry, they are usually looking for someone to blame. When angry people cannot find someone responsible for their anger, they tend to blame God. They may say things like, "If God was good, he would not allow bad things to happen."

For God to override, however, it would require him to take away the free will of people who act in a certain way ... that causes circumstances ... from which others become angry. To pursue this discussion, we would need to go outside of our subject and discuss the nature of God. This would take us away from our focus on the process of anger and managing anger.

Internal forces are feelings such as guilt, a sense of helplessness, unrealistic expectations, aimlessness, and low self-esteem (Walters, 1981). When the external conditions meet these internal feelings, the likely outcome of these combined factors is anger and some form of destructive behaviour.

For me, there seems to be too many factors to consider for us to deal with anger effectively. We need a fresh approach and a different understanding that will help us to process circumstances when we become angry. I know this from personal experience.

Since my early childhood, I had a problem with anger, and this continued into adulthood without an understanding of what caused me to become angry. I became a Christian at age 30 and a minister at age 38, but I still had anger issues. My denomination sent me for counselling, which helped a lot, but this did not deal completely with my anger problem. At age 46, I had some ministry with a group known as VMTC (Victorious Ministry Through Christ) and this gave me a final breakthrough.

As I journeyed along the pathway of healing, God was revealing to me what I am about to share with you. The central part of this teaching is a diagram of what I have called 'The Anger Cycle.' The phrase "anger cycle" comes from Walters' book (1981, p. 43). This book was immensely helpful to me and enabled me to start changing. However, the anger cycle described by Walters is not really a cycle at all. It is more like a flow chart.

I am indebted to Walters for much of my understanding of anger, but the way God has led me is very different. If you have read Walters' book, you will see much of his terminology in my work. However, our process is different. It is not that I disagree with Walters, I just see a different path for the cycle and a different way of processing anger. In the end, we both come to the same conclusion that the way to solve anger is through forgiveness.

The reality is: unforgiveness is linked to hatred. We normally hate someone when they have done something that breaks our belief system. Perhaps, they may frustrate a goal we have which prevents us achieving our desire. Sometimes, they devalue us by doing or saying something causes others or ourselves to think less of us or the things or life forms we value. Nelson Mandela has been credited with saying: "Hating someone is like drinking poison and expecting the person you have the problem with to die," although most are uncertain of its origin.

Forgiveness is extremely important as it leads to peace. Charles Stanley (2014) said: "Unforgiveness is an emotional bondage that consumes minds with memories of offences, distorts emotions with revenge and fills hearts with churning unrest."

> *"Unforgiveness chains us to the past, poisons the present and keeps us from what the Lord has for the future."*

Forgiveness enables us to reach our full potential. The opposite is also true. I really like the following quote, made by an anonymous author, that succinctly states: "Unforgiveness chains us to the past, poisons the present and keeps us from what the Lord has for the future."

We become hurt, and the hurt becomes anger.

During the review process I was privileged to be introduced to a young woman who is a Christian counsellor/psychotherapist. She rightly pointed out to me that people who have experienced trauma, grief, anxiety, or depression need to have their primary issues sorted out before anger can be addressed. I have not written about methods of dealing with anger in these cases as I am not qualified to do that. People who suffer from trauma, grief, anxiety, or depression including PTSD and (Post Traumatic Stress Disorder) or CPST (Complex Post Traumatic Stress Disorder) should seek help from a qualified psychotherapist counsellor. This young woman does not wish to be named as she says that the information is readily available in books and on the internet. I have included what she wrote because it explains the details in a more succinct and clearer way than I would be able to with my limited knowledge of psychology.

All scriptures come from
The Holy Bible, New King James Version.
Copyright © 1982 by Thomas Nelson, Inc.
However, when I comment on scripture, I use Australian English
which is sometimes spelled differently to
the American English of the NKJV

ACKNOWLEDGEMENTS

I will be forever grateful to the ministry of Rev. Graeme Cann, at Elkanah; my counsellor, Rev. Dr David Wilson, at Kingsley College; a book entitled *Anger: Yours, Mine and What To Do About It* by R. P. Walters (died, 2021), now out of print; the ministry of Victorious Ministries Through Christ; and the Christian and Missionary Alliance denomination. God has changed my life through these influences. I particularly owe VMTC a debt of gratitude because it was there that I found the value of what God had been teaching me as I used the cycle of anger ideas in ministering to others.

I would not have been able to get this manuscript to print without the capable and diligent work of Alison M. Dench who edited my book and helped me through the editing process. Her dedication to her work was inspirational and her advice was always helpful. Without her, this book would never have reached production. Thank you, my friend of many years.

Thank you, Rev Dr Kenn Iskov, my first and best Pastor, my friend and mentor, and the author of the Foreword. You have encouraged me since the day you led me to the saviour of my soul. Your early teaching and guidance have helped me to grow spiritually and has shaped me to be the man I am today.

Thank you also to my friend Rev John Laughlin who suggested I get Ali to edit my work. Thank you to my son-in-law Rev. Dr Peter Laughlin who, along with Rev. Graeme Cann, encouraged and inspired me to continue writing this book.

Thank you Lyn Cook and daughter Cheree who designed the cover and the illustrations. Your dedication and service to the Lord is an inspiration to me.

Thank you, Shirley Towner, for the final edit of the manuscript. Your help was invaluable and you are a blessing to me and so many others. Your reward is in glory.

Most importantly, I want to thank my wife, Veronica, who has stuck by me through the bad times and who has been my faithful companion these many years. Thanks for the chapter on living with an angry person. Thanks for your love, inspiration, support, and encouragement to complete this work. I have loved you from the first time I met you, and I still do.

I also want to thank the people on my launch review team who have given a different perspective and helped to make the book what it has become. My sister Lee Gunson, my brother-in-law Jack Busch, my son Rev MIchael Coman, my son in law Rev Dr Peter Laughlin, Rev Dr John Soper, Rev Dr Kenn Iskov, Rev John Laughlin, Craig Woodburn, Shirley Towner, Rev Ian Cullen, Rev Dr Rod Russel- Brown, and Vicar Rev Will Orpwood.

CHAPTER 1

My Journey

I was born in Melbourne on the fifth of November 1946. I had an older sister Beverley who was born in 1940. For the first four years of my life, we lived in Western Victoria. My dad was working as a dozer operator in the forestry industry which required him to move to various timber towns. When I was four we moved to Eildon about 140 kilometres northeast of Melbourne. We lived in my great-grandfathers' two roomed shack on the bank of the Goulburn River. My dad started as a dozer operator working on the new Eildon Dam until he was promoted to foreman on the crushing plant. Our house was demolished to make way for the new spillway so we were moved to Ninth street and then to Centre Avenue.

For as long as I can remember, in my early life I was a rebellious child who regularly got into trouble with those in authority. My first memory of conflict with such people was on my first day at school. I was five years of age, and my mother had walked me the 100 metres to the school at the bottom of our street. She told me I would be alright, and she would pick me up after school finished. As I walked around the corner onto the verandah, I came across two boys from grade three who were throwing rocks at the lights along the verandah. I told them they would get into trouble for doing that, and they told me it was allowed. I asked if I could play too. They said "okay," so I began throwing rocks at the lights, but hit nothing. The next thing I remember is the boys were gone and the headmaster had caught me.

He took me into his office and hit me six times with his strap. My sister who was in grade six in the next room heard me screaming and ran into the office and snatched the strap from the headmaster and took it to the woodshed where she chopped it up with the axe. I was too frightened to tell my mother what had happened because I thought that I would get into more trouble and get another belting. My sister did not tell anyone about the incident because she also thought she would get into trouble.

On my seventh birthday I had a party and because it was on Guy Fawke's Day I was given fireworks for presents which mum kept in a bucket, telling me not to touch them without supervision, meaning when my dad got home. Another gift I received that day was a book called, "Bonzo Goes to the Moon." On the front of the book was a picture of a dog riding on a sky rocket. I thought that this was a great idea so I ignored my mothers' instructions and took the largest rocket from the basket and held it in the fire until the wick caught alight and then aimed the rocket at the moon and held onto the stick until the rocket had burnt out. My right hand was very badly burned and my mother smothered it in butter which was the home remedy at the time but it was a bad remedy because it made the damage worse. I was rushed to the doctor who said that he would have to amputate my fingers. My mother said, "No, what else can we do?" I spent the next couple of months with my mum soaking my right hand in warm salty water every two hours. The treatment was excruciating but today my hand shows no evidence that it ever happened. My disobedience was very costly and could have been even worse had the doctor amputated my fingers.

One day during the following year I was visiting our next-door neighbour who I called Aunty. Aunty and mum were good friends. She would sometimes invite me into her home and would say, "I have something up my sleeve for you." It was usually a book or biscuits. This day, I went into her house and asked her if she had anything up her sleeve for me. She told me I was a naughty boy and, if I did that again, she would tell my mother. She told me I should not ask for things but wait for gifts to be given. Later that day, she came over to our house for a cup of tea, but I supposed she was going to tell my mother. As a result, I became very angry and this developed into rage.

I determined to get even and pulled the earth wire off the house which was attached to a piece of galvanised steel water pipe. As she came out our back door, I swung the pipe, intending to hit her on the head. My mum saw me and yelled, "Look out!" She ducked, I missed and got a belting for my bad temper. It turned out that Aunty never did tell my mum what I had said to her.

About this time, I and my brother Terry who was fifteen months younger than I started to go to a boys' club. We would run around in a circle in the theatre and the instructor would yell at us to keep our knees up. When he considered that our knees were not high enough, he would lash our bare legs with a leather strap. I now know that this was brutality.

When I was in grade three, my family moved from Eildon, to Wallgrove in outer western Sydney. In Victoria, they started teaching cursive writing in grade four, but in New South Wales it was introduced in grade three. We moved in October and, as I could not learn quickly enough, I was failed and kept down. My younger brother, who was 15 months my junior, was promoted to the same class as me. He was put in the higher part of the class, and I was put in the lower part. I felt humiliated.

When I was 11, we moved to Melbourne where we lived with my dads' brother for a year. One day as a joke my uncle hung me on the door by hooking my belt on the door knob which was one metre two hundred millimetres off the floor and told me that he would let me down if I asked, "Please Uncle let me down." I considered that this was unjust because I had done nothing wrong to be punished like this so I refused. I hung on the door knob for a couple of hours refusing to ask to be let down when my father came home and asked what I was doing hanging on the door knob. When he was told why I was there he gave me until he counted to ten to ask to be let down or I would get a belting. I gave in on the count of nine and was let down. I was very upset over the injustice of this event.

We moved again to Tantangara in the Snowy Mountains and I began grade six at the new primary school. The building had one room and an enclosed verandah. Grades one to three were in the main room and grades four to six were in the verandah. There were only six kids in grade six. I came fifth out of six children in the final exams. We all went to Monaro High School, but the girl who came sixth was put in a higher class than me. The class I was put into was a dummies class. There were four levels in first year of high school. Level one was 1A and 1D for professional studies. Level two was 1B and 1E which was considered the normal level. Level three was 1AC which stood for Alternative Course. Level four was 1C2C which was made up of children who had failed year six of primary school and were considered to be just staying until they turned 14 when they could legally leave school. I completed first year and we left a couple of months into year two.

Our family moved to Melbourne for a few months and then out to Forrest where we went to Colac High School one hundred and fifty kilometres west of Melbourne. At Colac High I was made to do French because it was a compulsory subject. The other children, along with my brother, all had nearly two years of instruction and experience; but I knew no French at all. I ended up getting 3% for French. Again, I felt humiliated.

The following year, we were back in the Snowy Mountains and Monaro High School where I passed my Intermediate Certificate. However, because of the system at Monaro High, I had to repeat the third year of High School at the normal level. The following year I was 16 years old and in a class with kids who were mostly two years younger, and my younger brother was a grade ahead in fourth year. I was humiliated and reacted the same way as before. That year was difficult for me as I had reached the place where I was serious about doing well at school, whilst most of the kids just wanted to misbehave and fool around.

One day, early in the year, I was working hard in a history class, but the students were in an uproar because the teacher had lost control. She screamed at the class and said we all had to do two pages of extra written homework. I put my hand up and, when I was spoken to, I told the teacher I was not going to do the homework because I had not been talking. I had been working. She said she did not care what I was doing; I would do the extra homework like everyone else.

The next day in the history class, the teacher told the students to put up their hand if they had not done the homework and half the class put up their hands. She then proceeded to ask each person why they had not done it. Most of the others gave lame excuses that she accepted, but when she came to me, I told her I did not do it because I was not guilty. There was a heated exchange between her and me which ended with her swearing at me, and me responding with a rude and inappropriate reply implying she was wanton. She was understandably upset and sent me up to the headmaster who gave me six hits with the cane and threatened me with expulsion if it happened again. I told him I did not want another chance; he could stick his school and I was not coming back. That was my last day at school. I had reached the end of what I could bear from unjust teachers. The humiliation and injustice had brought me to a place where the anger in me was explosive.

I expected that my dad would send me back to school but he did not and gave me a job working for the construction company he worked for, where he was the superintendent of the concrete batching plant and the crushing plant. I worked for Utah Construction at Island Bend for 15 months and mostly enjoyed work although I was probably a headache for my superiors.

A friend from my class in high school joined the Navy and came to our town where his father now worked. I fell in love with the uniform and the romance of Navy life and applied to join up. I was accepted and was at the Navy Training School at Cerberus, in Victoria, for ten weeks. During my time there, I really enjoyed life. I was unaware of the seriousness of my attitude to people in authority and my inappropriate response to correction. The more they tried to impose obedience upon me, the more I resisted, and the angrier I became at the treatment they gave me. They made me do something called jumps where they told me to wear a certain code of dress and report to the office. When I reported to the office the leading seaman commanded me to change my dress to another code after which I had to report to the office again. This went on for several different codes of dress until my locker was a shambles and my clothes were strewn all over my bed after which a locker inspection was called in five minutes. This was not enough time to rearrange the locker and I would fail the locker inspection and incur more punishment. An added problem was that I was supposed to run between my billet and the office but I began to walk to show my disapproval. After ten weeks, I was dismissed for failing to adjust to good order and naval discipline. I was again humiliated and thought the treatment I had received was unjust.

I was too ashamed to go home, but I had known only the Navy and home. So, I went home but felt I could not stay. This is because I felt a failure and did not want the constant scrutiny of my failure by so many people who knew me.

My dad knew someone who was a boss on the building of the National Library in Canberra who was willing to give me a start. I moved to Canberra and, in the next three years, my attitude and growing anger was responsible for the fact that I could not hold down a job. I had 14 jobs in the first year and 42 jobs in the three years I was in Canberra. My rebellion to authority was extreme.

I travelled with a friend halfway around Australia before I was conscripted into the Army to do National Service. When I was conscripted, I was working at Mount Goldsworthy as a rigger. Before I left for the army my parents gave me a party for my twenty-first birthday which would be a month after I was conscripted. That night the manager of the mine told me that when I got out of the Army there would be a job waiting for me at the iron ore mine.

I arrived at Puckapunyal on the fourth of October 1967. I was in constant trouble with those over me. The way the army dealt with problems like me was to punish the whole platoon. This often put me offside with the majority with whom I lived and trained. Once, I was beaten so badly by another soldier that the first aid people asked me if I had been hit by a truck. In retaliation for getting the platoon extra duties some of the men came to my bed at night and tipped a bucket of kitchen slops over me and fled. Another time it was urine and another time they threw my mattress out in the rain. I retaliated by being late for parade to punish them for what they had done so that they would get extra duties. This was a never-ending cycle only broken because we were all posted to corps training.

I was posted to Engineer Training School, Casula near Liverpool in Sydney.

Whilst I was at Casula, I had an incident where I hit another man who had provoked me by hitting me with his transistor radio. I had irritated him and, when he hit me, I punched him on the chin. He received four stitches. I was exonerated by our platoon commander and it was ruled as self-protection because he hit me first. His mate threw me in the river as revenge. I came out of the water and attacked him but he was waiting for me and knocked me out. When I recovered, I tried to fight him but the others pulled us apart but I vowed to get even. When this mate was about to go on the flying fox, I put a loop in the retrieval rope about halfway and fixed it to a star picket which I drove into the ground. When the flying fox got halfway across the river, it came to an abrupt halt and the board holding the three men flew out and dumped them in the river. My revenge was complete.

I also had begun to travel to Melbourne to see the woman who would become my wife. The problem was: I broke all the rules travelling interstate without a leave pass and not doing the guard duty I was assigned to. I had paid others to do my duty but, for some reason, they did not do it. I was caught and punished by extra guard duty and by being confined to the barracks. At this time our training was finished and I was posted to the Reinforcement Holding Wing awaiting deployment to Vietnam. When my previous commander tried to punish me for my disobedience my new commander of RHW said, "No one is going to punish these boys because they are going to Vietnam to fight for their country.

I did jungle training in Canungra near the Gold Coast in Queensland to prepare me to go to Vietnam. I got married whilst I was on pre-embarkation leave. Two days before I was scheduled to leave Australia, I was told I had been reclassified because of a hiatus hernia and would not be going overseas. I was really upset, but there was nothing I could do about it. I was posted to Western Australia where my wife was living, and I became an army driver with 22 Construction Squadron at Karrakatta.

I remained in the Army for another year during which time we bought a house in Cottesloe. We moved to Cottesloe four days after my eldest daughter was born.

This is where the violence started in our relationship and was to continue for the next eight years which was very damaging to our relationship. The violence was intermittent but was nonetheless destructive and wrong.

One day, we had an argument about something I can no longer remember. We were in the kitchen at our home in Cottesloe. I clenched my fist and told my wife I could hit her to which she replied, "Go on, then." She pushed out her chin and closed her eyes. I swung my fist intending to punch her, but a voice spoke to me in my mind saying, "If you hit her, you will kill her". I pulled the punch and swung around and punched the refrigerator, smashing the knuckle of my little finger. The next day, my hand had swelled up to two or three times it's size, so I went to hospital. I had the broken bone removed and my hand was put in a splint.

Another time we argued, my wife beat me on my chest, and I responded by slapping her. She fell down the step into the kitchen and split her head open on the corner of the fridge. That night she went to work at King Edward Memorial Hospital where she worked as a midwife, and they put four stitches into the cut on her head.

I worked as a contract cleaner, cleaning display homes and, on this particular day, I had asked my wife to help me because I was tired. She refused, so I took my eldest daughter and prepared to leave home. My wife came running out to the car with our second daughter in a bassinet which she put on the back seat, and she got into the front passenger seat. As we drove along beside the railway, we argued. My wife opened the door whilst the car was in motion. I stopped, and she got out and I began to drive off. Something caught my eye, and I turned to see that my wife had the back door open and was trying to take the bassinet out of the moving car. I braked and got out and ran around the car. I hit my wife knocking her to the ground and, every time she tried to get up, I knocked her down until she stopped trying to get up. I put the bassinet back in the car and put my wife into the passenger seat, then drove to my in-laws' house where I dropped her off with the children. When I got home from doing the cleaning, my wife was at home. Her mother had told her, "You married him for better or worse; go home and make it work."

When I got out of the Army, I sold life insurance for a year and then real estate. After that, I started my own cleaning business. At 26 years of age, I did a course with American Health Studios and became a masseur. Then, I bought a health studio called the Oxford Health and Beauty Centre. I also lost my licence because of accumulated demerit points, due mostly to speeding which was an expression of my rebellion to authority. Life became difficult with no licence, so I applied for a job at Mount Goldsworthy Mining and was given a job as a face shovel greaser. However, the job was boring and I became impatient to do work that was more satisfying to me.

I moved to Finucane Island six weeks later where, after 18 months, I became a leading hand plant operator with a crew of up to 12 men. For the first six months my wife stayed in Perth and then joined me on the Island. We lived with my parents for a year and the arguments continued although on the whole, our relationship was better.

After I had been in the north for two years, we moved to a farm near Dwellingup, 100 kilometres south of Perth, where I worked in bauxite mining with Alcoa. At Alcoa, I worked on the powder crew and then began operating an old excavator on rough and undulating ground. I did not like being thrown around inside the excavator, so I would purposely break the machine to obtain a rest from operating. One day, the excavator broke in half because of the abuse I gave it. I was not a good employee and, during this period, I stole gear and explosives from the company.

Life on the farm was pretty good but there were times when I reacted badly. One time my wife had served my meal. We were arguing about something, now long forgotten, when my anger boiled over and I said some mean things. I turned over my plate full of food onto the table and then threw the plate at the kitchen door. It smashed into pieces. Unfortunately, my children were also present and suffered trauma. Afterwards I cooled down and I forgot the incident, but permanent mental scars were left in my children and my wife.

Two years after we came to the farm, we became believers and followers of Jesus. My life began to change dramatically and the violent aspect of my character was gone although it was close at times. Our relationship slowly improved but it took about five years to repair the damage done by my bad responses to my anger. My wife had lost trust in me which took time to be restored. My journey of anger was over and my journey from anger had begun.

We became involved in the ministry of the church. The church ran Daily Vocational Bible Schools in the school holidays as an outreach to the children in our town. They were very successful. One day, the Pastor approached me and asked if I would organise the next DVBS. I agreed but, because of my lack of maturity and sensitivity, began telling various people what I wanted them to do in the next DVBS. A lot of the people did not want to be told to do things but wanted to be asked to help. They got upset and complained to the Pastor, telling him they would not be involved if I was leading it. The Pastor approached me and told me he had decided not to run the DVBS the next school holidays. I found out what had happened, and became very angry.

I began ranting to my wife describing how I was going to slash the tyres of those who had rejected me. I was planning my revenge. As the days passed, I got worse. My wife became concerned that I would carry out the threats I had been making and called the pastor who said he would speak to me on Sunday. My wife told him she thought Sunday would be too late as I was likely to do something I would regret before then. The pastor came that evening and we talked about forgiveness. Just speaking about the issues eased the situation and, later, I stood in church and confessed my anger and asked for forgiveness. What shocked me the most was the comments from some in the congregation who said they hated me for the way I behaved. It has become clear to me that these people also had anger issues that were unresolved.

I became more involved in the church and its ministry and I began to study theology by remote courses and began preaching. Our pastor went to study in the USA and we were left without a pastor for over six months. I was teaching the Adult Bible Study every week and preaching three times a month, twice in our church and once a month in Harvey, a small town 40 kilometres further south.

At Christmas time 1980 I preached a sermon in which I questioned the validity of the King James Version of the Bible but, when I apologised a person in the church asked that I be kicked out of the church. My apology was misunderstood and I was asked by the elders to stop preaching until our new pastor came and could sort things out. The new pastor came but he listened to others who criticised me but he never asked me what happened. I was hurting so I went to our Perth church and sought some advice. The elders reported my actions to my pastor who called me to his office and angrily told me to stop airing his dirty laundry all over the state. The preaching and teaching ban stayed in place for eight months but I was told that I could still do maintenance on the church buildings. I found this time very difficult. I was continually asked to preach in Harvey and a small aboriginal church in Pingelly. I asked the pastor what I should do and he told me it was up to me so I went to Pingelly but was chastised by him when I returned.

We went to Canberra where I began Bible College in February 1982. I struggled in my studies but managed to pass and by the fourth year I was getting the occasional "A".

In my third year of college, I began working with a Vietnamese church and the following year they asked me to be their pastor.

In my first year of college my son disobeyed his mother and involved me by asking my permission to go to a friend's house when his mother had already said, "no". I sent his sister to get him and when he returned, I was in a rage and gave him a belting that marked his bottom. I had broken the cardinal rule of never giving punishment when in a rage. I greatly regret this incident but I cannot undo this action. I am now ashamed of this belting and my son and I have resolved this matter. I apologised and asked for his forgiveness which he gave when he was 18 years old after his first year at Bible College.

When I was being interviewed for a Pastor's License, a member of the board caused my wife to cry and I told him that if he did it again that he would be sorry. He asked me if I was threatening him to which I replied that he could take it any way he liked but if he made my wife cry again, he would regret it. The president intervened and a conflict was avoided.

After I graduated, I accepted a call to pastor at Footscray with a small group of 25 people. It was hard work especially when the national board required me to be the major breadwinner. My wife earned a good wage as a nurse. The extra income was handy but the combined workload at church and secular work became heavier for me.

I received a command to meet with the national board of our denomination at Denny's for breakfast. Some of the people in the church had complained to our national office about my aggressive behaviour. At the breakfast I was told that they just wanted to encourage me but the opposite was my reality. A member of the board began to read from my monthly reports where I had asked for prayer because I was struggling to work at a secular job and run the church. He ended up saying that he did not see any gift of pastor in me nor did he see the gift of evangelist and he questioned whether I had any gifts at all. The president told him to back off but I was devastated and left in a daze and went into deep depression for about three weeks. I was told to go to a retreat centre called Elkanah, about an hour out of the city, to have an assessment. I did not like being directed to do this, but I had been told if I had not arranged the trip to Elkanah within a month, I would lose my pastoral licence.

My wife kept asking me if I had made the booking and reminded me the time was passing. I felt like burying my head in the sand, hoping it would all go away. However, I knew the national board of our denomination had meant what they said, so at the last minute I made the appointment.

When we arrived at Elkanah, my wife Veronica and I were told to do a survey (called the Taylor Johnson Personality Profile) which had over 250 multiple choice questions. It took us a few hours to complete. We were also told to do a survey (known as the Edwards Personal Preference Test) on each other of 125 multiple choice questions. We were then interviewed together, and the assessor showed us a graph that he had plotted our answers on and said that in the area of conflict I disappeared off the top of the chart and my wife disappeared off the bottom. He said, "Let me tell you what happens when you have conflict. When you have conflict, your wife runs away and says, 'I don't want to talk about it.' You chase her saying, 'Let's talk this out.' You keep chasing her and she keeps running away". I said, "That's right." He said that he had only seen one other graph like mine and the man was a double murderer in Pentridge Gaol. He said had I not become a Christian I would definitely have become a murderer. He also said I had a serious anger problem which could be resolved.

I was referred to a counsellor in a Bible College in Melbourne and, again, I procrastinated, feeling like I was being picked on. At that stage in my life, my identity was bound up in me being a pastor, so I felt compelled to do the counselling. My wife agreed, at the first meeting with the counsellor, to come with me; but she, herself, did not have counselling. She was moral support for me. The counsellor had me read a book by R. P. Walters called *Anger: Yours, Mine And What To Do About It*. This is the best book I have ever read on anger, and it is the foundation of all that I know about it. Sadly, this book is now out of print.

I was profoundly changed by the application of the principles in this book, but it did not deal with the root of the problem or help me understand the process of anger.

After three years at Footscray, I went back to Western Australia. We settled in Gosnells and we began meeting with the local Alliance church where after a year I became part of the eldership team.

After an evening service in 1990 I found out that some of the boys in our church along with my son who was 15 at the time had been throwing rocks at the Hindu temple next door to the church and one of the rocks had broken a window. I became very angry but did not punish my son but spoke to him about his behaviour. I made him come with me to the temple and confess his part in the rock throwing and offer to pay for the broken window. The way I was dealing with my anger now was becoming better.

The senior pastor left and the assistant pastor became the senior pastor. At one of the elders' meetings one of the elders proposed that I should become the assistant pastor and a vote was taken and the vote was a unanimous yes. Three weeks later I was contacted by one of the members of the church who told me that the senior pastor had betrayed their trust. I tried to resolve matters by speaking to the senior pastor but he denied any wrongdoing so I went to the president who told me that he did not believe me. When the senior pastor went to the president, he was advised to sack me which they did. I was disappointed and angry about this but I was beginning to leave it in God's hands so my response to anger was improving.

I was involved with VMTC (Victorious Ministry Through Christ) in Perth, Western Australia. It was my fourth school and, at that school, I was expecting to be released as a second or support minister, so I could begin to do this ministry with other people. At the last meeting, I was taken aside and told I was not being released because I had a problem with authority, but they were releasing my wife. I was devastated! I felt rejected and devalued and became angry.

I went out the back of the retreat centre, where there was a treed area, and began walking around. In my grief and anger, I began to yell at God telling him I had done the best I could and that I was okay. I challenged him to show me what the problem was.

It was then I had something like a video clip in my mind of that first day at school. The Lord told me when that had happened, I had made a decision that people in authority were not just and were not worthy to be respected or obeyed. I suppose I saw for the first time what I was really like. Over the next three weeks, the Lord took me through the rest of my life and showed me how this problem had grown in me.

Each time I had encountered an injustice I had decided that people in authority were not worthy to be obeyed or respected so I became more hurt and more rebellious. My rebelliousness and anger began to make sense to me. I could see that the combination of my level of anger and my rejection of anyone in authority was the cause of my considerable problems in relating to people.

I asked to have some ministry for this where I confessed my sin and forgave those who had wronged me. I was delivered of a spirit of rebellion and it was a new day. Previously I would not wear a seat belt because I said it was my right to do what I wanted. By the age of 46

I had lost my licence for the second time for loss of demerit points. I began wearing a seat belt and became conscious of my speed and other road rules. My anger was directly linked to the incidents that caused me to be a rebel.

Soon after I was asked to pastor a new church of Vietnamese because I had worked with a Vietnamese church in Canberra for two years whilst I was at Bible College. I agreed and began working with the Vietnamese church and it grew but the national board refused to give me a Pastoral License because I had been sacked as an elder. I was angry at this treatment especially when I was told to just pastor the church without a licence. I felt used and not honoured or respected. Because I had no official position and therefore no authority it made pastoring this church more difficult. The Lord was teaching me how to respond when I became angry. Because I believed that I was called of God to pastor I continued but I continually had to deal with my resentment and bitterness. The violence was over but my internal struggles continued.

I left the Vietnamese church after two years and became the assistant pastor at another Australian church. It was while I was at this church that God gave me a vision of the anger cycle. I drew a model of this and it has developed over the years into the diagram included in this book.

Three years after I was sacked, the elder who sacked me came to my house and told me that I was right and they had been wrong and that the senior pastor had been asked to leave. After he had left, they had discovered what had been happening. It was good to be exonerated but it was never made public knowledge.

I spent six years at the Australian church and was then called to Kalgoorlie where I pastored for 12 years before I retired. Whilst I was at Kalgoorlie the Lord revealed the five responses to anger to me.

I had been involved with Victorious Ministries Through Christ since 1990 and this ministry required that I have ministry at each school which was every six months apart from 18 months when my pastor would not give permission to attend a VMTC school. During the late 1990s I began using the information I had learnt to minister to people with a root of bitterness in VMTC but was asked to stop using it until the leadership had examined what I was doing. I wrote a letter to the president of VMTC in June 2000 where I outlined the ministry I had been doing. Six months later I received a letter approving the ministry of dealing with roots of bitterness. When I was using this ministry at VMTC I was often asked to teach others how to do it because it was so effective in the ministry.

As I went through the process of dealing with my anger and rebellion, God taught me some helpful information. I know now how and why I get angry. Yes, I still get angry, but the outcomes are much better now. I also know how to deal with the anger, how to avoid harmful anger outbursts, and what to do so that I am not so easily provoked to angry outbursts. Finally, I have learned how to resolve issues in an appropriate way.

It took 15 years for me to work through the process of dealing with the anger, resentment, bitterness, and violence, to the place where I gained a clearer understanding and better behaviour. For me and for those who have an anger problem it is a journey, but our time on the journey may be very different. There is no instant cure. On this journey we learn how to deal with our beliefs and our unacceptable behaviour. We change our beliefs and our behaviour when we understand what we do and why we do it and the consequences of our actions.

CHAPTER 2

Anger

What Is Anger?

Anger is a greatly misunderstood term. I hear people speaking about righteous anger and unrighteous anger. The way I see it, anger is an emotion ... a very necessary emotion. It is simply an emotion like joy, sadness, fear, or hate. Anger is neither righteous nor unrighteous because it is just a feeling.

When I ask people if anger is good or bad, I generally get a negative answer. Most people see anger as being bad. This is a misconception. Anger is good and without it we are impaired and unable to respond appropriately in many situations. It needs to be clearly understood that when I say that anger is good that I am not saying that wrath or rage is good, but that anger as an emotion or a feeling is good because it can and should motivate us to righteous action. Some people would call it indignation. Anger in itself is not bad but when we choose wrong responses, we will do wrong things. So, it is not anger that is bad but our wrong responses to the emotion of anger.

> *Anger is a God-given emotion we use to preserve our beliefs, our goals, our worth, and the worth of other people, things, life forms, and our environment. It is an emotion of God and is, therefore, an emotion of those made in his image.*

Because everything about God is good, anger is good. Good things or emotions can be used for evil. God has given us the free will to choose how we respond in all circumstances. This does not mean everything we choose to do is good or right, but it simply gives us the ability to choose our responses. **We ought to choose good** and right responses because then we will always have the best outcomes.

The Bible and Anger

The Bible, in its original language, tells us to be angry but places some conditions around it: "Be angry **and do not sin**." (Ephesians 4:26 quoting Psalm 4:4). This means that we should become emotional about wrongs such as injustice, violence, or anything that has a negative effect on ourselves or others. The Bible is truth and would not tell us to do something bad or wrong. Why would God tell us to be angry? This is a command from God. To see or hear something that is unrighteous or violent or exploitative or damaging to anyone else or to yourself, should stir up emotions in us. One of those emotions may be anger. One of the reasons God tells us to be angry is because he, himself, gets angry.

The Bible has many examples of God being angry. God gets angry with unholiness, injustice, unbelief, and disobedience. If anger is sin, then God is a sinner. God is good, holy, pure, and just; and this means he has never sinned. Therefore, anger is not sin. Neither is it sinful to remain angry, for God remains angry with all sin. If God gets angry, then anger is good.

Unlike God, however, we are not perfect, nor do we manage our anger as well as he does. We are made in his image, so we have the capacity to be angry. Indeed, it is necessary for us to become angry at the things that God becomes angry with. We also have the capacity and the need to make right choices when we become angry.

Jesus, God's son, also got angry. He was angry when he called the scribes and Pharisees "hypocrites" and told them that they were like whitewashed tombs (Matthew 23:27–33). He was angry when he sat down and made a whip of cords and drove out the money changers and the merchants from the temple (John 2:13–16).

Jesus was angry at the religious attitude of people. "Then he said to them, 'Is it lawful on the Sabbath to do good or to do evil, to save life or to kill?' But they kept silent. ⁵And when he had looked around at them with anger, being grieved by the hardness of their hearts, He said to the man, 'Stretch out your hand.' And he stretched *it* out, and his hand was restored as whole as the other. (Mark 3:4–5)

Be angry, but do not sin.

The Effects of Anger on the Body

Anger has both a physical and an emotional effect upon us. Dr Harry Mills writes,

"As you become angry your body's muscles tense up. Inside your brain, neurotransmitter chemicals known as catecholamines are released causing you to experience a burst of energy lasting up to several minutes .... At the same time your heart rate accelerates, your blood pressure rises, and your rate of breathing increases. Your face may flush as increased blood flow enters your limbs and extremities in preparation for physical action. Your attention narrows and becomes locked onto the target of your anger.... In quick succession, additional brain neurotransmitters and hormones (among them adrenaline and noradrenaline) are released which trigger a lasting state of arousal". (2005, para. 3)

To read the rest of Mills' informative article, click on the link in the References page.

Simply stated: when we get angry and do not respond appropriately, the anger continues to build; and it is then we get the effects Dr Harry speaks about.

To confuse anger with wrath is a mistake. Wrath is extreme anger that is not checked and is allowed to manifest with rage, which is mostly a choice, but in most circumstances is a bad choice. Anger is necessary to enable us to respond in appropriate ways when incidents occur that need a response. If we cannot get angry, we are unable to respond to violence or attack or wrong behaviour.

Anger can be cyclical.

Anger can be cyclical. It follows a pattern which I have called 'The Anger Cycle' (see page 29). The cycle begins with an **incident** which triggers anger.

There are three anger triggers: Beliefs, Goals, and Value.

Three Incident Types That Trigger Anger

Incidents take many forms, but there are three types which act as triggers. These are: (1) anything that breaks our **belief system**; (2) anything that frustrates our **goals**; (3) and/or anything that **devalues** or cheapens our personal **worth** or the worth of other people, animals, things, or even the environment. These triggering incidents usually cause us to be hurt emotionally. In turn, this hurt often results in the emotion of anger. Let me explain this further.

Beliefs

We are offended and hurt when our beliefs are compromised. When something happens or when someone does or says something that goes against what we hold as essential truth, we may become angry. You may say you are upset, or you did not like what happened. You may be saddened or even appalled by an incident, but the response is the emotion of anger. These beliefs may be factual or even untrue, but the important thing is, you believe them to be true. When these beliefs are broken by other people or even ourselves, we become hurt or feel hurt; and this hurt becomes anger.

All people have personal standards. That is, we have principles, rules, and ideals that are intrinsic to everything we do or say or expect in and from others and ourselves. These make up our moral standards and the rules by which we live. When these are transgressed by others, or even ourselves, we can become angry.

We may have a philosophy that one good turn deserves another. However, if we do another person a good deed and when the other person has the opportunity, they do not reciprocate, we can be hurt and become angry. We may have a standard that a married person does not commit adultery, so if the person we are married to commits adultery, we are hurt and get angry. We may have a standard of achieving "A"s academically and fail to reach that standard, so we become disappointed or hurt and become angry with ourselves. We may even look for someone else to blame, like the teacher for making the exam too hard.

We even have beliefs we are not aware of that would be more properly termed 'expectations' than beliefs. Some of these expectations are realistic, but some are not. The important thing to remember is not whether our expectations are realistic but that we can become angry if our expectations are not met. This can be a difficult part of relationships because beliefs often change in people and society, and what was considered wrong can be deemed to be right, and what was believed to be right can become wrong in the eyes of society or even governments. In this book, we are dealing with people and our responses to the things and situations where we become angry.

Goals

All people have goals. Goals dominate our lives. We cannot live without them.

We have our life goals. These are not our dreams but the things we have determined to do, what we have decided we will achieve. Sometimes these goals have not been verbalised but are an inner commitment. When our goals are prevented from being achieved, we are disappointed; and that disappointment often becomes the secondary emotion of anger.

We also have function goals. Function goals are the things we want to achieve to just live what we would consider to be a functional life. For example, what we decide to wear each day is a goal. When we find the clothes we wanted to wear are in the wash or at the dry cleaners, it is a possible conflict incident. When we burn the dinner that was supposed to be a culinary masterpiece, we may become angry at ourselves for not cooking it right. We may become angry at the new oven that does not cook like the old one or at a recipe that did not work out. We may even be angry at the spouse or guest who came later than was expected so that the dinner was ruined.

We get frustrated and hurt when someone or something prevents us from achieving a goal that we might have. This goal may or may not be reasonable. It may be a simple goal of just getting home. It may be a goal of scholastic or sporting achievement. It may be a goal of wanting to see the end of a movie or a TV show or the end of a football game. It may be the goal of completing a project or spending time with our friends or going to the shops. In fact, it can be any of a myriad of goals that we might have, simple or difficult, necessary or unnecessary, achievable or even impossible. It matters not what the goal is. What matters is our expectation of achievement. When that goal is denied us, we become hurt or frustrated or both. This hurt or frustration manifests itself in the emotion of anger.

Sometimes our anger results in a combination of trigger incidents. Guilt, or often false guilt, causes us to feel somehow responsible for negative circumstances and can cause us to become angry at ourselves, even if we cannot see how we are responsible. A sense of helplessness can cause anger because we think we should be able to prevent bad situations, but for various reasons we cannot, and that leaves us feeling powerless. Aimlessness and low self-esteem can have a similar outcome causing us to become angry. Homelessness can cause us to become angry even if it was our own decision to leave our home and live on the streets.

People have asked, "What about grief, doesn't it cause us to get angry?" Grief may cause us to become angry but it may just cause us to be sad. Grief is a sadness that is our response to tragedy. We think whatever the tragedy was it should not have happened. This is a frustration of our goals because we probably wanted the person to go on living. Grief may be a breaking of our belief system because we think the person should not get sick or die. We are never prepared for the death of a loved one, or for a major sickness in ourselves or in people or pets we love or care about. These also are a frustration of our goals or the breaking of our belief system in that we don't want ourselves or loved ones to be sick or to die.

Many people go into a marriage expecting marital bliss but when relationships are not what they expect, a kind of grief is experienced. This was our situation. We felt this grief because our unspoken desires were not met. These were unspoken goals, unspoken beliefs and an unspoken value that was not met in the short term. Grief has many aspects but boils down to one or more of the triggers which may bring anger, frustration or just deep sorrow.

Value

We may get hurt or offended when someone or some situation causes us to lose our self- image or self-value. Asians call this losing face. We all have a value or worth. A person's personal worth is the value they have placed on themselves.

All people have a value on themselves. This is not a value that has been calculated but an innate value that is built into every person. It is most clearly seen when that value is abused by another or even oneself.

For example, few people think they are stupid, but they have a value which sees themselves as bright or intelligent to varying degrees. When someone says we are "stupid" or "dumb," we are immediately offended and hurt by the comment. Our response is to become hurt and then to become angry.

Our value is God-given for we were all created in his image. God created us with value, and he showed the immensity of this value when he allowed the sacrifice of his son, Jesus, for us. In essence, God has said the payment of the life of Jesus gives us the value of God, for that was the payment made to redeem us.

Scripture tells us we were purchased or bought at a price (1 Corinthians 6:20). This price or value is the life of Jesus which was paid for us when he died on the cross. Our value is the life of God the Son, and there is no higher value. When we buy something, we pay an amount that is what we value the item as. Usually, the value is what we pay until the value either increases or decreases. God's value on us is eternal because he gives us eternity as a gift when we trust in him. This value is extended to all people while they live for God who treats all people alike by giving rain and sunshine and seasons to bless us. The real difference comes after death when the sheep are separated from the goats.

When this God-given value is devalued or questioned, we are hurt, and this hurt manifests in the emotion of anger. When we hear comments like, "you'll never amount to anything," or "you are worthless or useless," or "you can't do anything right," we are hurt because we have been devalued. Our intrinsic value has been denied, and we are understandably hurt. Even if the comments are true, we may still become hurt because we feel devalued.

Many of the statements and actions that cause us to be hurt—because they devalue us—are made by people who are not necessarily conscious of the effect they have on us. Most people do not know how much damage is done when the value of a person is questioned.

As I have previously stated, we can include (as well as our own worth), the worth of anything: a tree, a habitat, an animal, or another human being. God has given mankind the job of looking after the earth and its environment. Genesis 1:28 reads: "Then God blessed them, and God said to them, 'Be fruitful and multiply; fill the earth and subdue it; have dominion over the fish of the sea, over the birds of the air, and over every living thing that moves on the earth.'" So, when the worth of anything that God has created is abused, we may become angry about the abuse or the devaluation of that thing or person created by God. Mankind was given care of the world but when we see the creation God made being damaged by neglect or by profiteering from its bountiful resources, we may become angry because the value of the environment has been abused.

When this value is challenged, we become hurt, and anger, disappointment or even annoyance is our emotional response to the hurt we feel.

In thinking about anger, it has occurred to me that some people do not even know that they have become angry. Because anger is an emotion a whole range of feelings would come under the classification of anger.

A close friend of mine after reading the draft of the book in order to help me by giving me feedback told me that she had to deal with becoming hurt so that it would not develop into a root of bitterness. This got me thinking about what other feelings would come into that category. Some of these feelings are obvious but others are much milder but I believe that they are all forms of anger.

If I am **aggravated** or **outraged** or **annoyed** or **offended** or **provoked** or **irritated** or **vexed** or feel **hurt** it is a precursor to anger. If I am **distressed**, I am **saddened** about something or **displeased** or **wounded** and found something **distasteful** or something that **bothered** me or **grieved** me or **disturbed** me I am what I would call pre-angry. The outcome could still be unforgiveness which is a sign of a bitter root which produces anger that could become rage. When any of these feelings ring true for you then you need to look a little deeper and ask the question, "Will this feeling lead to unforgiveness and a root of bitterness?" On the other hand if you find that it was just a feeling and did not lead to something negative, then just let it go.

Our response to anger is a choice.

In these incident types, we can see that a belief, goal, or value is violated in some way. The primary emotion is anger, hurt, frustration, or disappointment. We become angry because we have been hurt. We become angry because we are frustrated. We become angry because we are disappointed. At this point, we have done nothing wrong because what we do with our anger is what determines whether we do wrong or not. When we choose to let our anger become rage, we may become violent, critical, sarcastic, judgemental, or nasty and raise our voices or even shout.

Anger is an automatic chemical reaction of the body

Please note that **anger is an automatic chemical reaction of the body**. No person or situation can make us angry. Anger rises in us because of one or more of the anger triggers that sets off a chemical reaction in our bodies.

The Christian counsellor/psychotherapist whom I referred to in the preface wrote "The current understanding of psychologists is that, like all emotions, anger begins as an 'automatic' physiological response to some sensory input (e.g., sight, sound, smell, taste, sensation to the skin including temperature change, and internal sensations such as hunger or fatigue) that triggers our nervous system to activate further physiological reactions. For anger, the autonomic nervous system initiates a 'flight, fight, freeze, or fawn' nervous response which affects other physical responses including the release of various hormones, changes to blood pressure and distribution, digestion, visual and auditory system changes, etc. What creates the outworking of this 'automatic response' instead of a different 'automatic response' is individual and includes factors such as our genes, our current state of physical health (including our nervous system), the environment in which we are at that time, our emotional state as we receive the sensory input, the intensity of the sensory input, our past experiences (including the physical, social, emotional and spiritual factors) to similar input, etc. How our brain then interprets this sensory input and our reaction then provokes thoughts. These thoughts are influenced by all of the previously mentioned factors and can also be influenced by our conscious thinking choices".

The Anger Cycle

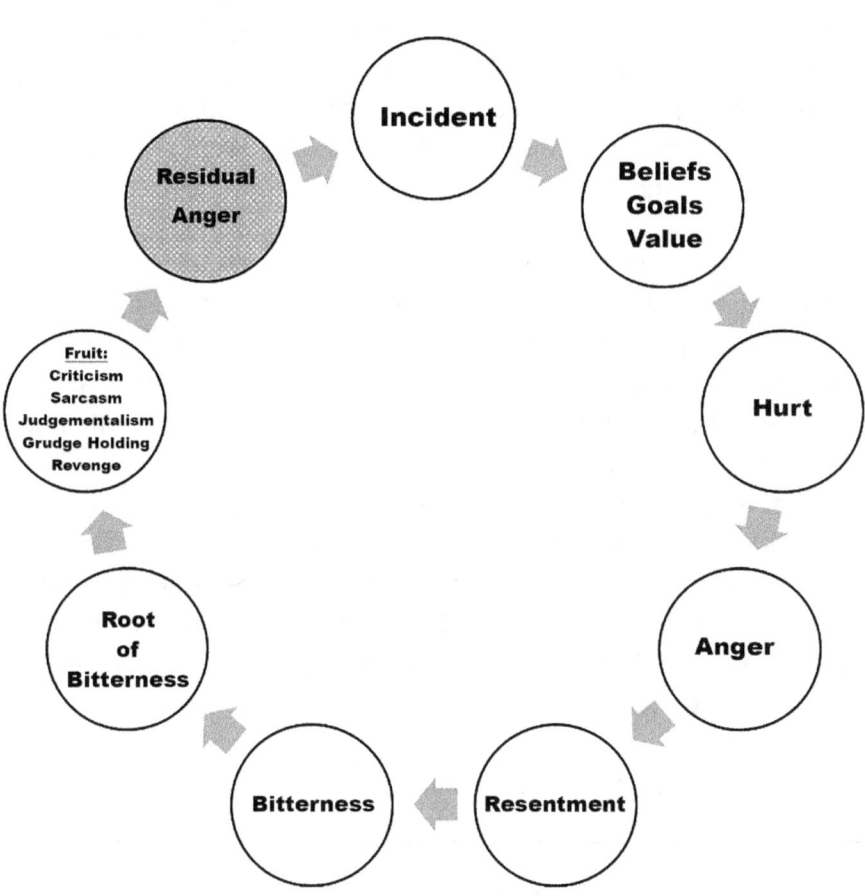

Responding to Anger: The Anger Cycle

When we don't deal with our anger appropriately, we become **resentful** (see previous page). When resentment is not dealt with appropriately, it becomes **bitterness**. When bitterness is not dealt with, it begins to grow as a **root of bitterness**. Hebrews 12:14-15 tells us, "Pursue peace with all people, and holiness, without which no one will see the Lord: looking carefully lest anyone fall short of the grace of God; lest any **root of bitterness** springing up cause trouble, and by this many become defiled." We can see in these verses that God wants peace for us with all people but the root of bitterness causes trouble and defiles us and causes us to be a hindrance to the joy and happiness of ourselves and others.

The root of bitterness has **fruit**: sarcasm, criticism, judgementalism, and grudge holding. It may also be manifested in raised voices, obscenities, or other acts of violence to ourselves or to others, animals, or things. When the issues causing a root of bitterness are not resolved, we enter a state of **residual anger,** which is a growing state of anger. When the next incident occurs, the cycle begins again, but the level of anger is elevated. These will be explained in more detail in a later section. What I mean when I say fruit of the root of bitterness, is a manifestation or behaviour that indicates that the root of bitterness is there. The root itself is not visible but is internal or psychological. The manifestations or behaviour is visible and shows us what is not visible, that is the bitter root.

Between Anger and Resentment

There are five different ways we respond to anger: Reaction, Repression, Retreat, Resolution, and Release.

These happen on the anger cycle between the steps of "Anger" and "Resentment" (see page 29).

There is no implied order to the responses. There are five different ways we can respond to feelings of anger.

Reaction

The first response is reaction, because it is a reaction to an incident—like an explosion, letting everything boil over. Most often other people cop the brunt of this rage. This response is what most people think of when they hear the word "anger," but it is only one of the responses to anger.

This reaction might be physical like breaking something or hitting something or someone. Reaction is destructive in all its forms. The reaction may be verbal which seeks to be destructive through criticism, sarcasm, or insults directed towards those who have caused the hurt. Reaction can be likened to a dormant volcano erupting. When the eruption occurs, everything around the volcano is hurt or destroyed, but the volcano settles down, because the pressure has been released and becomes dormant again. When a person who is angry chooses reaction, the eruption may be verbal or physical. Those who are around the erupting reactive person will suffer from the verbal abuse or the physical abuse, or both, and will be scarred by the eruption. However, the erupting person will often feel calmer because the pressure has been released and that person cannot understand why other people are still upset.

This is clearly seen in the incident I spoke about on the farm where my wife had prepared a meal for me and I became angry during an argument. I reacted wrongly by throwing the dinner on the table and smashing the plate as it hit the door. Afterwards I quickly became calm but my wife was still hurting and my children had been traumatised. Both my wife and my eldest daughter became afraid at my outburst of rage. Both chose to suppress their feelings, so that they would not further irritate my irrational behaviour and exacerbate the situation.

Repression

The second response is to suppress our feelings. This type of action is most common when in the presence of a superior or a boss, to retain employment. It is also the most common response by those who believe that reaction is inappropriate or sinful. To maintain dignity or favour amongst others, repressors push their feelings of anger down, so it appears the person is coping.

Ongoing use of suppression can lead to health problems, as the adrenalin created by anger if not used will attack its own body. Like the person who is reactive and explodes, the repressor will implode inwardly and cause damage to self. The result is nervousness, mental problems, and health disorders like high blood pressure or heart problems. People of a quiet disposition will often choose this type of response because it avoids conflict. Others who may use this response are those who believe all anger is wrong or sinful. In my marriage, my anger has mostly been reactive whilst my wife responded by repressing her anger. This caused a problem with the way we communicated, and neither of us understood the other's response or perspective.

My wife tells of the way that she coped saying that she retreated out of fear and repressed her true feelings because she thought expressing her anger would make matters worse. She felt unable to express herself clearly so said nothing during the times of conflict. She was too ashamed to talk to others about what was happening in our relationship so she hid it from everyone, even her family.

Retreat

The third response is to run away or retreat. When we find it too difficult to repress our anger—or if the opponent is more powerful and the damage received is not worth the resistance—retreat is the wisest course of action. If we put physical distance between ourselves and the one who has caused our anger, it is much more difficult to make poor choices regarding the way we respond; but when the issue is important, it is not worth the safety of retreat. Retreat is a very important option for those of us who would normally react or blow up or lose it. As a person who reacted violently, I found that when I was removed from the confrontation, I cooled down quickly and came to a place of remorse. Then I was willing to admit my wrong actions and words.

It is also very important that where possible the person who is the object of aggression should try to retreat to put space between the aggressor and him or her self because it is harder to do damage to each other if there is distance between them.

My wife said, that during an argument she would retreat out of fear because she could not or would not talk about things. She would disappear into the bedroom and lay crying on the bed. This was her safe place where she could sort things out in her own mind and gave me the space to calm down. Continued confrontation increases the risk of violence therefore it is prudent to leave when you can safely do that.

Resolution

The fourth response is to resolve the problem. This is the best response, but it is not always achievable. Resolution happens when we can communicate with the person or institution responsible for our anger. In this way, we can work out why we have become angry, find a solution for the conflict, and implement the solution in our lives.

I have been working on resolution for the times I became angry with the situations I found myself to be in during my life. Many of them cannot be resolved because some of the people involved have passed on, and some will not accept responsibility for their part in incidents that happened. I have not been able to deal with others because of the lack of an appropriate opportunity to talk through the incidents.

Release

The fifth response is to accept the situation and to let it go. If the issue is resolvable, we should not let it go, but things like road rage often cannot be resolved. Also anger at someone who dies often cannot be resolved and must be let go. A deceased person is not able to be communicated with, so the problem becomes one sided. In this case, the only action that can be taken is by the person who is still living and has been affected by the incident or multitude of incidents and that is to let it go, to release it.

Sometimes those who are involved in the incident are unwilling to be part of the healing process. They may not see things from your perspective or may even think they are not responsible or did nothing wrong. It would be wrong to try and force our perspective upon others, so the right thing to do is let it go and accept that it may never be resolved in a way that is satisfactory for us.

Sometimes people cannot be part of the healing process because they are full of bitterness and have a root of bitterness. They may consider it too painful to process any further. Of course, this attitude may change at a later time because we know resolving issues benefits all parties. However, the hurt is often so deep and the emotional scars are so raw that it is difficult to continue to process. The truth of the matter is that the person or persons may not want to forgive because what they may want is revenge and retribution. This only leads to deeper hurt. Jesus said unless we forgive others, he will not forgive us. Forgiveness is the only real cure. It is the only action that resolves our issues and opens the door to peace and healing.

Release seems like an easy solution, but it can often be hard to implement. To hold onto our unforgiveness does far more damage to us than letting it go. When this is our last resort, it is essential for our own mental, physical, and spiritual wellbeing.

Responding Appropriately

All these ways of response may be appropriate according to the circumstances. To put it another way, all responses are not always appropriate, but sometimes each one is appropriate or right. As you read the following examples this will become clearer.

Reaction

Most of us would agree that violence is not an appropriate response for us, but there are times when we need to respond physically. Think of a scenario where you are walking in a park or even down your street and an assailant attacks your spouse. The assailant would most probably not respond to calm words, so there is a need to defend your spouse: either to overcome the assailant or to enable an escape from the situation to call the police. In this situation, reaction of a physical nature would be entirely appropriate.

Repression

In general, repression is not good for our health because when we become angry the body produces adrenaline. When the adrenaline is not used up, it will attack your own body causing high blood pressure, heart problems, and nervousness. However, there are times when we need to repress our anger. Imagine you are stopped by the police for a traffic infringement. If you are nice to the police officer, it may not escalate. However, if you are rude and abusive, it may well end worse for you. Repression is the right response if the situation is inappropriate to show wrath or malice and an explanation or reason will not work.

Here is another example of repression. Little Johnny is at school and is falsely accused by the teacher of talking in class. Johnny knows if he tries to defend himself, the teacher will say he is talking back, and he will be kept in for recess. Johnny is angry he is being blamed for something he did not do, but he says nothing because he does not want to miss out on recess.

We need to manage our responses well when we become angry. There are many times we need to suppress our emotions of anger but without sin.

I am reminded of a Rotary Dinner that my brother Terry invited me to where I was seated opposite an industrial counsellor, and the conversation turned to anger and anger management. He told me of a time when he was called out to a warehouse to assess a young man with an anger problem. The counsellor sat near the counter and watched the young man as he worked. The young man was abrupt and rude to customers whom he served, but when the manager came and stood behind him, he was a model employee and treated the customers with respect and good manners. However, when the manager went back to his office, the young man returned to his abrasive manner. Later, during a tea break, the counsellor went into the crib-room and sat with the young man. He asked him why he was rude to the customers. The young man said he could not help himself because he was just an angry man. The counsellor reminded the young man of the time when the manager stood behind him and he treated customers well. He replied, "You cannot be rude to the customers when the boss is watching because you'll get the sack." The counsellor responded, "So you can control your bad temper."

Our response to anger is a choice we all have

The young man saw for the first time he had a choice, and his behaviour was his decision. After that, he changed the way he treated customers. There is always a reason for our anger responses and, usually, the reason for the behaviour needs to be addressed before change can happen.

After thinking about this young man, I am inclined to conclude there were deeper issues in his life that were the basis of his angry attitude just as there were in my life. This young man would have benefitted from good counselling, helping him discover the real root of his problem which, in turn, could have brought resolution and healing.

Retreat

Retreat is often a good response to our anger, unless there is a more appropriate reaction such as resolution—or defence of ourselves or our loved ones or others whom we can deliver from danger.

Retreat separates us from the incident, so we can think about it and form an appropriate response. Going into another room or going for a walk around the block is often enough space to clearly think through our actions. Sometimes more space is needed and separation from the incident or the people or person involved. This gives an extended time for consultation or counselling which can be beneficial to all parties involved. When someone is prone to violent outbursts, it is always necessary to be separated, so damage to ourselves or others does not occur. This is often the case with domestic violence where the parties need space, one for protection and the other for counselling and reform.

Retreat or, to put it another way, delay, is the right response when there is a possibility that our response will be the wrong one or will cause us or others more trouble.

Consider this situation. Little Johnny knows that Jimmy was the one who was talking, but if he says something to the teacher, he will be called a "dobber." If he says something in class to Jimmy, he will be guilty of talking in class.

Consequently, Johnny decides to delay his response. During recess he says to Jimmy, "Why didn't you own up?" The two boys talk it out and remain friends. When Johnny goes home, he tells his mother what happened, and his mother rings the school. She speaks to Johnny's teacher, assuring him that Johnny was innocent. The next day, the teacher apologises to Johnny in front of the class, resolving the problem. Even though Johnny's mother told the teacher who the child was who was talking, the teacher wisely chose not to say anything to Jimmy so as not to betray Johnny. Instead, he kept an eye on Jimmy to catch him red-handed.

Resolution

Resolution is always our goal with conflict, but it is not always possible because some people do not want a relationship to be restored for various reasons. We should always respect the wishes of others, but we should always keep the door open for resolution. Jesus prayed for his people to be one as he and God the Father are one (John 17:11). Jesus also said if we wanted to be forgiven for our indiscretions, we will have to forgive others for theirs. Resolution will nearly always involve forgiveness. Unforgiveness is usually at the root of our developing anger cycle and is the reason for a root of bitterness in us. The only way to complete the healing of a root of bitterness is through forgiveness of the incidents that caused the hurt, anger, resentment, and bitterness. None of us are perfect and faultless. If we want others to forgive us, we should be willing to forgive others otherwise we are hypocrites and we do not want to be known as hypocrites.

Resolution is always the right response where it is possible. If Johnny had had a good relationship with his teacher, and his teacher had trusted him, he would have been able to resolve the issue right away.

Release

Release is the last resort because the very best result is resolution. As I have said earlier, resolution cannot always be achieved. Release is hard because we often want justice, which means we want some form of punishment for the person who caused our pain. We are often double minded when it comes to forgiveness because we think we need to be forgiven for everything, but we also think there are times when forgiveness should be withdrawn or withheld from others. Not only do we think that forgiveness is to be withheld, but we believe there should be some form of punishment.

Mentally, a lot of people believe in a form of purgatory where people must suffer until they have paid for their crimes. This type of thinking does not take into consideration that when Jesus died on the cross, he paid the price or penalty for all sin for all time. On the cross Jesus cried out, "It is finished." What he meant is that our sins and misdeeds are completely paid for. There is no longer a need to pay for the sin. Payment is complete. Paul writing to the Colossians told them that their trespasses or sins were forgiven and all accusations against them were erased, wiped out or rubbed out. Truly sin has already been paid for and all that is left for us to do is to forgive. (Colossians 2:13-14).

When releasing a matter or an injury or hurt, we need to remember we have been forgiven all by God, and we need to pass this forgiveness on to others who have offended us. God's promises to us are, "I will be merciful to their unrighteousness, and their sins and their lawless deeds I will remember no more". (Heb 8:12). Also, "He will again have compassion on us; he will subdue our iniquities. You will cast all our sins into the depths of the sea". (Micah 7:19). Putting these two verses together we find that God says that our sin is buried in the deep sea and he will remember them no more.

The reality is that much of what we release is not able to be resolved satisfactorily. To not forgive or release leaves us in a state where just the memory of those incidents or hurts leaves us emotionally scarred, but if we can release them and forgive, they are gone, and we are free of the pain. In my introduction I quoted an anonymous person who said, "Unforgiveness chains us to the past, poisons the present and keeps us from what the Lord has for the future." Release changes this. It sets us free from the past, removes the poison from the present and opens the future for us to explore in peace.

Release sets us free from the past, removes the poison from the present and opens the future for us to explore in peace.

Acceptance and release are appropriate responses when issues are impossible to resolve.

Acceptance is essential because now it is history and cannot be changed and the only thing we can do with it is to release it and let it go.

If you are angry with someone and the person dies, the matter is usually unresolvable, so the best thing to do is to forgive the person and let it go. To be unforgiving will only leave us full of bitterness and residual anger.

> *"The discretion of a man makes him slow to anger, and his glory is to overlook a transgression" (Proverbs 19:11)*

If someone cuts you off in the traffic, you may never see them again to talk about it. So, instead of being resentful and bitter about it, it is better to accept nonresolution and drop it. Forgiveness does not mean that the other person is innocent or right but that you have chosen to leave the incident in the past.

Forgiveness means we will no longer hold the issues against the person and will leave the judgement up to God who knows the true state of events. Because he is just and righteous, justice will eventually be done.

However, in the end resolution and release must take place, or the relationship will be damaged and friendly relationships will be impossible.

The answer to resolving the anger cycle is simple but often hard to apply. When the incident is truly forgiven, change is immediate. However, forgiveness is not always as easy to accomplish as saying, "I forgive you." Do not give up. The mind knows that this is right but often, especially when the offence is considered serious, the heart continues to grieve. The heart often needs time to heal from an emotional wound, so the process of forgiving must be repeated many times to be effective as time is needed to heal the heart and the emotions.

Responding Inappropriately

When an incident happens, we feel hurt. If we can fix the hurt, the issue may not go any further. However, if the hurt is not remedied, it becomes anger, and anger becomes resentment. Now we are entering into the other stages of The Anger Cycle.

Let me explain with some personal stories that I have shared earlier on pages 1-2.

As a five-year-old, I was subjected, by the headmaster, to the punishment of a belting for throwing stones at the verandah lights. I made a decision at that time that was to change my life for many years—in fact for 41 years! When that happened, I made the decision to believe (probably incorrectly) that people in authority were unjust and not worthy to be respected or obeyed. I resented the treatment I received and the person who gave me that treatment, and I assumed all people in authority were the same. I was too frightened to tell my mother and father because I knew I had done wrong. If they had known about the incident, I expected I would receive more punishment from my parents. When I eventually told my mother in my late 40s, she told me she would have defended me (and I suspect she would have given the headmaster some of his own medicine). If I had told my mother and she had gone to the headmaster, I may have had an apology which may have resolved the matter. That did not happen, so I became resentful and then bitter about the incident. As time went on, I grew a bitter root and became sarcastic, critical and judgemental of people in authority. Every time there was an incident with people in authority, I became hurt, angry, resentful, and bitter; and the bitter root grew; and the rage in me got worse. The reservoir of unforgiveness, which I have called "residual anger" grew, and the area of darkness (literally rage) in me became greater.

My real problem was rebellion or disobedience. When I was seven years old this disrespect of authority nearly cost the life of my aunty next door, if it had not been for the quick reactions of my mother.

It nearly cost me my right hand which the doctor wanted to amputate all because I did not obey my mother when I took the skyrocket and tried to go to the moon.

My anger increased. When I was nine years old, and I was kept down in grade three I was bitterly disappointed, and more so because my little brother was put into the higher Grade three and I was put into the lower Grade three. My goal to go into Grade four was frustrated. I felt devalued by the teachers and my belief—that if you were in Grade three you should go into Grade four—was broken. A similar thing happened when I went to high school. I placed fifth in a class of six children, so when I was put into a lower class than the girl who came sixth, I became hurt, angry, resentful, and bitter again.

Resentment

Resentment is a feeling of displeasure or indignation at some act, remark, or person causing hurt, injury, or insult. Resentment usually results in an attitude towards those who have caused our hurt. We become suspicious of their ongoing intentions regarding us and we do not trust them. On the other hand, the feeling of resentment is an opportunity to forgive those responsible for our injury. If we do not forgive others, our resentment, if left to fester, will develop into bitterness.

Bitterness

Bitterness is acidic, which is a good description for this emotion. Something acidic is something that burns, and bitterness does more damage to the person holding it than it does to others. Bitterness is destructive because it rehearses the wrongs perceived to have been done. It often imagines conversations with the offender. It loves to tell the stories of hurt that have been experienced. Bitterness is toxic and seeks to turn others against the offender.

The result of bitterness is, we become uncomfortable in the presence of the offenders and constantly feel like we are going to be attacked. We don't trust the offenders. We feel vulnerable in their company. We are looking for more issues to happen that will strengthen our case against them. Bitterness will continue to become worse unless it is confessed and the issues are forgiven. Otherwise, bitterness will develop into a bitter root. For those who do not have a faith you may feel that this confession stuff is not for you but what I am saying is that there is a need to admit that we are being affected by bitterness and that if this attitude continues it will develop a perspective that will lead to a hardening of our emotions and a psychological stance that will end up causing us more pain and heartache.

This is what happened to me in 1977 when I became a believer in Jesus and became involved in the ministry of the Church. I was asked to run a Daily Vocational Bible School in the school holidays as an outreach to the children in our town. I was a young Christian and handled the organising badly telling various people what I wanted them to do. The people resented being told what to do instead of being asked for help so they refused to work under me. The pastor wisely cancelled the event but I became angry because I knew what had happened and felt judged unfairly. In hindsight I think the pastor did the right thing but I was immature then and did not understand the full situation.

In my anger I chose to be resentful and then bitter and then began to plan my revenge. My wife became concerned at the threats I was making and wisely called the pastor to help which he did and averted actions that I would later regret. My anger had developed into a root of bitterness. The rest of this episode is on page 10-11.

The Root of Bitterness

The root of bitterness is sown the moment an incident occurs and the issues remain unforgiven.

Every time an incident occurs and proceeds around the anger cycle— incident, hurt, anger, resentment, bitterness and then a root of bitterness—the root grows. In the diagram, on page 44, we can see how the root of bitterness begins very small but, as each unresolved incident happens, the root gets larger.

The root is an area of darkness in our being. When we do not choose forgiveness and reconciliation, we resist the grace and light of God. This area is outside the influence of the Holy Spirit because it is our free choice to continue in unforgiveness. God never forces his will on us but, instead, allows us to reap the consequences of our choices.

The reason why this bitter root is so dark is because it ignores the command of God to forgive, so it becomes rebellion against God and his word. Unforgiveness is a serious sin that limits God's forgiveness to us. He tells us that if we do not forgive others neither will he forgive us (Matthew 6:15).

The Root of Bitterness illustrations

The Root of Bitterness

In this illustration we can see that the root of bitterness begins very small and has little effect on the person but as it grows the mood of the person changes to unhappiness and discontentment. The root has gone from the heart to the mind and is now affecting the thoughts. Unforgiveness is the major difference and that causes criticism, sarcasm, a judgemental mindset, the holding of grudges and a desire for revenge. In this unhappy state words are often harsh and the voice is often raised.

In this illustration we can clearly see that the root of bitterness begins small but eventually takes over the whole person the other thing that we see in this picture is that the light is overtaken by darkness and joy is overcome by sadness and an ill temper.

The only antidote to a bitter root is forgiveness and repentance. Confession, repentance, and forgiveness can remove the bitter root and restore relationships. The moment we forgive, it brings us back to God's system for resolving issues. It allows the light and love of God to operate in our lives again, which brings healing and forgiveness to us. When the issues are resolved, we become free of the root of bitterness. Then, we have the freedom to forgive more easily, and the reservoir of residual anger decreases. In this way, the anger cycle is eventually broken as we continue to forgive.

> *Forgiveness can remove the bitter root and restore relationships.*

To find out the cause of the bitter root, it is necessary to ask, "What did the person, company, institution, school, or organisation do to hurt you?" The offended person then needs to forgive the one or ones responsible for the hurt. When this is done, the root will die. It is possible to take yourself through this process, but it is best done with another person. Very few people can minister to themselves in this way. When we do this with another person, that person can ask us questions that we may not ask ourselves. Another person may also be more objective than we might be because he or she is not as emotionally involved as we are.

Some issues, like sexual abuse, may take longer to forgive and heal. This is due to the very nature of the offence, and the very deep hurt and anger associated with this type of trauma. I stress that the same pathway is used in dealing with all types of anger trauma. In forgiving, we do not imply the actions causing the anger are okay, for they are never okay. Holding the feelings inside of us, only feeds our anger and rage, and renders us powerless to move on in our lives to be free. I repeat: all types of abuse are wrong, and we must become angry about these actions, but we must work out the issues of resentment, bitterness, and residual anger to gain freedom.

> *We must work out the issues of resentment, bitterness and residual anger to gain freedom.*

The Fruit of Bitterness

The root of bitterness produces evil fruit: sarcasm, criticism, judgementalism, revenge, and grudges.

As we dwell on our circumstances, we tend to become critical and sarcastic of people who have hurt us. We become judgemental and a desire for retribution grows in us. Finally, we may develop a grudge that colours our perspective and causes actions that we may not have entertained before.

The root of bitterness produces evil fruit.

It is very easy to see the presence of a root of bitterness by the sarcastic remarks, criticisms, and judgemental statements made about a person or an institution. The bitter root grows every time unresolved issues or situations arise. When the bitter root grows to a size where it is bigger than the love in the relationship, the relationship usually breaks down.

We can picture this breakdown in a relationship by envisaging two areas in our bodies of different shades. Whilst the area of love is dominant a relationship may survive but when the area of unforgiveness is greater than the area of love the relationship will most probably fail. This is much like an infection in our bodies. Whilst the body is able to resist the infection it will recover good health but when the infection is stronger than our body it may never recover good health.

The resolution of a root of bitterness is quite simple. We, ourselves, or a counsellor discerns the existence of the root of bitterness as evidenced by the unsavoury fruit listed above. Comments of revenge or the presence of a grudge, a raised voice, or obscenities are also clues. The root can be many faceted involving many people or it may only involve one relationship or one facet of a relationship.

As the issues are revealed and the instances where unforgiveness exists are made obvious, the counsellor should stop and ask, "Are you willing to forgive this person for the things that were done or said?" If the answer is "Yes," the person should try to remember back as far as possible and begin to pray or say, "I forgive (person's name) for (the offence)." Sometimes the anger is not sin, but the problem is with the sins of unforgiveness, resentment, bitterness, criticism, grudges, or plans of revenge. The anger develops into unrighteousness through this process. God promises us through the apostle John, "If we confess our sins, He is faithful and just to forgive us our sins and to cleanse us from all unrighteousness" (1 John 1:9). When a person who is not a person of faith in God is dealing with a bitter root the process is the same but our terminology may be different. When people who are not of a faith background want to deal with a bitter root, they can still voice forgiveness. They can say I forgive you for whatever the issue is. This is not necessarily a spiritual matter for an unbelieving person but a change in commitments to not continue to hold past issues against others. If this sounds like a bit of gobbledegook check out Dave's story in chapter 7.

When a root of bitterness is not dealt with through forgiveness, the bitter root grows after every incident and becomes residual anger.

Removing the Root

For a believer the root of bitterness is removed by confessing the unforgiveness involved and forgiving the person who is the cause. God does the surgery but it cannot be done until forgiveness is given. This does not have to involve the person who is the cause because it is our problem. We are carrying the unforgiveness and it is affecting us and causing us to be a person we do not really want to be.

For the person who is not a believer the process is the same but you may see it as throwing away the rubbish instead of God removing it.

> *"Do not hasten in your spirit to be angry, for anger rests in the bosom of fools" (Ecclesiastes 7:9)*

Residual Anger

Residual anger is the state of a person who has continually not dealt with unforgiveness and, every time this happens, the bitter root grows and the residual anger increases. This situation is detrimental to the person and is destructive to relationships. It sometimes causes demonisation (see Chapter 6 and Appendix 3). This state can become very dangerous to self and to others.

When I was visiting an aboriginal community out of Kalgoorlie I was invited to speak to a group of ladies about understanding anger. After I had shared the anger cycle with them one of the ladies said, "I got that residual anger." The treatment that aboriginal people have received over the years has caused many aboriginals to have high levels of anger over the injustices they have endured. These high levels of anger often bring with it domestic violence which in turn causes high levels of residual anger in aboriginal communities. Forgiveness is the only cure for this residual anger. The road to healing in these communities also needs to have an element of dealing with past trauma.

Today, wrath is present in our society and touches the lives of more and more people for lots of reasons. Violence is often on our TV screens. Many computer games are games of violence, making it difficult to separate reality from these games. The level of frustration in society is at an all-time high. To add to this, travel is often difficult because of volumes of traffic on our roads. People are used to everything being instant and, when ordinary chores take time, those people become frustrated. This frustration often becomes anger and then rage.

Most people are ill equipped to deal with the pressure and do not understand that forgiveness will set them free from the tyranny of rage and hurts and from the cycle of unforgiveness and the bearing of grudges. The result is a society with too many people suffering from roots of bitterness and huge reservoirs of residual anger. We simply categorise these people as angry men or angry women.

King Saul was such a man who became jealous of the praise given to David, and he envied David's fame and notoriety. Saul's anger rose and the resentment became bitterness. The root of bitterness grew in him, and his level of residual anger was dangerous. He tried on several occasions to kill David and even cast a spear at his own son when he had suspicions that Jonathan was helping David (1 Samuel 16:14–31:13).

CHAPTER 3

Responses to Anger

"Anyone can become angry, that is easy; but to be angry with the right person, and at the right time, and for the right purpose, and in the right way – that is not within everyone's power; and it is not easy."
Aristotle

The Usual Response to Anger

The Bible describes how we once responded to incidents before we became believers. Consider these two verses of scripture.

"Because of these things the wrath of God is coming upon the sons of disobedience, in which you yourselves once walked when you lived in them. But now you yourselves are to put off all these: anger, wrath, malice, blasphemy, filthy language out of your mouth" (Colossians 3:6–8).

"Let all bitterness, wrath, anger, clamour, and evil speaking be put away from you, with all malice" (Ephesians 4:31).

The behaviours that Christians are told to put off are the natural behaviours of the old person or the pre-Christian person. Not all unbelievers are unruly people. Many of them behave in a manner that is better than many believers. In dealing with the outcomes of anger, it matters not if we are believers or not. The process to resolution is the same.

These verses describe an incident to which there is a response of anger that becomes wrath and then malice. This is usually followed or accompanied by blasphemous words and filthy language. Hatred sets in and is demonstrated by spite, malevolence, meanness, nastiness, cruelty, and wickedness which become resentment in the heart and then bitterness that desires revenge. This is not a desire for justice but a desire to retaliate and hurt those who have caused the hurt or offence or who are perceived to have caused the hurt or offence. This sort of behaviour never resolves the problem. Retaliation often makes the situation worse than it is.

He who is slow to anger is better than the mighty and he who rules his spirit than he who takes a city (Proverbs 16:32)

The Biblical Response to Anger

The Bible, however, shows us a way to respond so the anger cycle in our lives does not proceed. We are commanded, "Be angry, and do not sin: Do not let the sun go down on your wrath, nor give place to the devil. Let no corrupt word proceed out of your mouth, but what is good for necessary edification, that it may impart grace to the hearers. And do not grieve the Holy Spirit of God, by whom you were sealed for the day of redemption. Let all bitterness, wrath, anger, clamour, and evil speaking be put away from you, with all malice. And be kind to one another, tenderhearted, forgiving one another, even as God in Christ forgave you" (Ephesians 4:26–27,29–32). And, again, "Be angry, and do not sin. Meditate within your heart on your bed, and be still." (Psalm 4:4).

Step One: Be Angry

We begin at the same place as everyone else with an incident when we are hurt and become angry. We need to become angry at the things God gets angry about. Getting angry is a very healthy thing to do. We need to be angry with injustice, sexual assault, child molestation, abuse in any form, animal cruelty, environmental abuse, and the list goes on. Remember God commands us to be angry.

Step Two: Forgive All

To not sin, there needs to be an immediate response of forgiveness for the incident, whatever it is. Thus far, we have not sinned; but as we think about the incident, the hurt comes back and we are soon in a state of unforgiveness, which is not helpful and **is** sin. I am not just speaking of a religious formula but a sincere process from the heart. This is further discussed in step eight.

Step Three: Retreat

Find a place that is away from others. In the Psalm 4:4 verse, it is "on your bed." We are removed from the incident, so we cannot do any damage and the situation does not escalate. This is referred to in the **Responses** to anger as "retreat." Meditate within our heart or, in plain English, think about what happened. It would be prudent to ask ourselves if we did anything that caused the incident. Did we contribute in any way to the incident?

Step Four: Meditate

Is there something we need to confess as our fault? Do we need to apologise for anything? The term "meditate within your heart" implies emotions, so we could ask the questions: "How did I feel? Was I offended? Do I feel wounded? Did I wound the other person?" How did the other person feel? Was the other person offended?"

Step Five: Be Still

Do nothing, be still, on your bed. Let there be time to process the whole event. When we get angry, we tend to want to do something. In some cases, like defending a loved one, that is a right response. Mostly when anger is triggered, it is wisest to take time out to consider a right and wise reaction and response. Before I had my counselling, I would chase my wife around the house trying to force her to talk about a conflict that we had. I did not know that she needed time to think about our conflict. I would have done well to be still. I would have done well to give her time to think through the issues and I would have done well to go away and think about the issues myself and also it would have given me time to cool down. At this stage the adrenalin is still racing around the body and will cause havoc if we try to communicate in this state.

Step Six: Do Not Let the Sun Go down on Your Anger

Do not let the sun go down on your anger. Wherever you can, resolve the matter before you sleep. This is good sense because if you have guilt about anything, you will not be able to sleep. If there is unforgiveness about anything, you will not be able to sleep. Of course, there are issues we become angry about that cannot be resolved before we sleep, but the principle remains that where we can resolve our anger issues, we should before we sleep. If the resolution will take longer, we can commit to writing what we are angry about. Then, it is good to choose someone whom we trust and to share with that person how we plan to resolve the issue, so that there is a plan before we sleep. Afterwards, we commit it all to the Lord (Psalm 55:22).

Step Seven: Do Not Grieve the Holy Spirit of God

We need to be careful we have done nothing to grieve the Holy Spirit. As the Scripture says: "Let all bitterness, wrath, anger, clamour, and evil speaking be put away from you, with all malice. And be kind to one another, tenderhearted, forgiving one another, just as God in Christ forgave you" (Ephesians 4:31). When we have been hurt, we find it most difficult to be kind and tenderhearted. We grieve the Holy Spirit when we behave in an ungodly manner. We always need to carry out God's ways in a godly manner, so the Holy Spirit is not grieved.

Step Eight: Continue Forgiveness Until It Is Complete

Forgiveness is also difficult when we have been hurt. We must remember it can be a process. The process often looks like unforgiveness because we may genuinely say the words that we forgive but, as we replay the incident in our minds, the hurt comes back. There is a need to repeat the forgiveness until we truly forgive unconditionally. When we speak to others about our choice to be angry, we often justify why we are angry, and we find ourselves repeating how someone has hurt us.

In this way, we become critical, judgemental, and sarcastic and we regurgitate the very issues we have forgiven. It becomes unforgiveness and then needs to be forgiven all over again. The Lord has shown me that when Jesus said to forgive "seventy times seven," he meant forgiveness is a process, and it can take 490 times to forgive for some things or events until they are truly forgiven. The term "seventy times seven" really means "infinite" which means to always forgive just as he has forgiven us. It means he expects us to forgive others, always, regardless of whether the person repents or not. We may never forget the painful incidents that happen to us, but when we work at forgiveness, we will be able to remember them without the pain and condemnation.

This is not really about the other person. It is about us, and about our attitude and our forgiveness of others.

How Do I Know When Forgiveness Is Incomplete?

I had a situation where I was hurt by a person and struggled to forgive him. I would find myself telling my story and being critical, judgemental, and condemning of his actions after saying, "Lord, I really do forgive him." At the time I prayed that way, I meant it, but my words condemned me and exposed me. My wife would later tell me that my words did not match my confession, that is, I said I forgave but my words condemned the person I was hurt by. This has been a common pattern throughout my life. In fact, I took 15 years to forgive one person. With the person in my story, it took three or four years.

When my wife challenged me, I would go back to the Lord and cry out to him and say "Lord, how long will it take"? The Lord spoke to me and told me when I could cry for his misfortunes and pray for his deliverance, the forgiveness would be complete. There came a time when this became reality for me, so I offer these following tips to help you forgive.

You Have Really Forgiven:

When you no longer criticise the offender.

When you no longer complain about the offender.

When you can sorrow for his or her misfortune.

When you can remember the incident without pain.

When you can point out the benefits you have gained by going through the experience.

No longer criticising the person with whom we have had an issue demonstrates that the root of bitterness connected to this relationship is dead. This also means that all the residual anger with this person is also dealt with. Not complaining about the person also tells us that we are now thinking of the person non critically and opens the door for compassion for any misfortune the person is going through. The lack of pain associated with the memory of a painful experience demonstrates that the issue is now in the past and has no bearing on the future. Finally, when we can point to valuable lessons learned from a past painful experience it shows that we are now being objective in relation to what happened and shows a growing maturity and godliness.

All conflict is an opportunity for our characters to be developed, and no character develops without conflict. The fact is: people do us a service when they bring conflict into our lives, though at the time, we do not think so. Forgiveness is perhaps the greatest asset we have, and we should use it often. I am not saying conflict is a good thing, but there can be good that comes from conflict if we are willing to learn and be shaped by a bad experience. God's word tells us: "all things work together for good to those who love God, to those who are the called according to His purpose" (Romans 8:28). This perspective can be a life changing experience for us that alters the way we look at all situations in our lives and reduces the likelihood of responding badly to the anger triggers.

CHAPTER 4

The Bible on Anger

The Bible presents anger as a strong feeling of displeasure of God and mankind. Anger is often mixed with hostility and hatred. In the Old Testament the most common word for anger is *aph* (apf) which comes from a root that means "to breathe hard." In the New Testament the term is *orge* (orgay) which is translated as "anger," "wrath," or "indignation" depending upon the context. God's anger is always just, but the anger of man often involves hatred and aggression. In the Bible, we see the full range of the expressions of anger—from a feeling or emotion to outright unrestrained wrath leading to murder.

The book of Proverbs includes wisdom about anger and angry people. Our anger journey in Proverbs begins with an admonition to guard our mouths or watch our speech because it may well preserve our lives. On the other hand, if we let our mouths run rampant in an ungodly tirade of inappropriate words, we may well suffer destruction (Proverbs 13:3).

We need to be patient and slow to anger, so we can understand what is really happening. This enables us to make the right response which may well keep us safe when an impulsive reply or action may land us in hot water and reveal our foolishness (Proverbs 14:29).

"A soft answer turns away wrath, but a harsh word stirs up anger" (Proverbs 15:1). One of the practices we can work on to make proper use of our anger is making soft answers. This is a learned practice and needs repetition and deliberate control of our emotions and our tongue, to bring harmony even in difficult and distressing moments. Harsh and inappropriate responses will often inflame our difficult and distressing encounters whereas soft responses will tend to calm the situation. Just the act of dropping our tone will convey the fact we are not being threatening but rather that we are being conciliatory. Loud and aggressive behaviour sends the message we want to fight, or we want to increase the conflict.

"A wrathful man stirs up strife, but he who is slow to anger allays contention" (Proverbs 15:18). A person who has lots of unforgiveness and, therefore, has a large reservoir of residual anger is a powder keg waiting to be ignited. Consequently, it is necessary to deal with any unforgiveness in us because when we have a forgiving heart it is much harder to stir up our emotions of rage or wrath within us. The person who is slow to anger is a person who has a clean heart, free of the unforgiveness that stirs our passions to react violently.

"A man of great wrath will suffer punishment; For if you rescue him, you will have to do it again" (Proverbs 19:19). The punishment the person of wrath will suffer is not just the penalty of the law for crimes committed against others. The unforgiveness that is stored in the heart that I call "residual anger" is a much greater problem than a financial loss incurred because of rebellion against authorities; and it will ultimately end in punishment from the law of the land. The greatest problem with stored unforgiveness is that the chemicals that are released when we live in a state of anger are detrimental to our health. (See Dr Harry Mills' comments on page 20).

"Better to dwell in the wilderness, than with a contentious and angry woman" (Proverbs 21:19). This applies to both genders. Contention has its roots in residual anger or unforgiveness. Living in the presence of contention and constant anger is wearing on our emotions and robs us of the peace and tranquillity we all desire. If we deal with the unforgiveness in our lives, we will go a long way to restoring peace and tranquillity in our lives.

"A prudent man foresees evil and hides himself, but the simple pass on and are punished" (Proverbs 22:3). The main emphasis here is to avoid angry encounters. When people become loud and aggressive, it is prudent to avoid them. The same can be said of difficult circumstances. If we know that certain circumstances cause us to become angry, it is better to avoid those circumstances than to deal with the consequences of them. In this way, it is possible to avoid the triggers that cause anger and life will be more peaceful.

"Make no friendship with an angry man, and with a furious man do not go, lest you learn his ways and set a snare for your soul" (Proverbs 22:24–25). This verse is more counsel about avoiding difficulties when we can. It is better to avoid some people who have anger-related problems than suffering the consequences of their behaviour. The other problem here is: when we hang out with people who tend to become furious, we can pick up their bad habits and end up being like them. We are better served if we choose well-behaved and peaceful people as friends, as they will be an influence for good and teach us good character traits. The final point made in this proverb is that relationships with furious people could well cost us our eternal life. Whereas when we make friends with people who are well behaved, it will help us grow more like the person God wants us to become.

"Scoffers set a city aflame, but wise men turn away wrath" (Proverbs 29:8). Scoffing is not a trait that Christians or anyone else for that matter should have, as scoffers are usually amidst trouble. Scoffing rips the fabric of peace apart and is the opposite behaviour of a Spirit-controlled person which God expects of us. Wisdom that comes from God always turns away from wrath and seeks peace.

"An angry man stirs up strife, and a furious man abounds in transgression" (Proverbs 29:22). We are to not only avoid angry people but, if we ourselves are like that, there is an urgent need to change. Transformation is not only necessary; it is also possible for any person whether they are Christian or not. An angry person is a person with a reservoir of residual anger and is always on the brink of trouble and strife. Residual anger will cause us to be furious often and will cause us to transgress when we should be law abiding. People like this are full of rage, literally looking for an opportunity to manifest their wrath because the pressure on a person to vent their anger to release the pressure is immense. In reality, the pressure can be released more effectively through forgiveness; and joy will be the result instead of rage.

New Testament teaching on anger

Our understanding of anger in the New Testament begins in Matthew 5:22 where Jesus is teaching about our attitude to others, telling us that if we are angry with our brother which is literally all other people, we are in danger of judgement. Jesus is OK with people who get angry with others for a just cause but the anger needs to be resolved with some positive action. The context of this verse is that of an ongoing grudge which is harmful to peaceful relationships.

In Mark's Gospel Jesus is concerned about people's anger at doing good on the Sabbath. He was grieved at their hard hearts and their bondage to religious practices that prevented good and righteous behaviour and he condemned this attitude. (Mark 3:4-5.)

In Luke's Gospel Jesus teaches us about anger in two parables. The first parable tells us that God is angry at people's refusal to respond to his invitation to come to celebrate with him and so invites anyone who wants to come including those who would not normally get invitations which includes the poor, maimed, lame, and the blind who were the discarded and despised of that time. (Luke 14:16-24.)

In the second parable about the prodigal son the anger is from the older brother about a gracious act of the father. We see the older brother exhibiting unforgiveness towards his brother and even accusing him of acts that are not proven. The father in this case is Father God who says that anger in this case is not right. (Luke 15:25-32.)

In John's Gospel we have two instances of Jesus being angry. The first is in chapter two where he is incensed about an improper use of the temple as a place of commerce. He makes a whip of cords and drives the traders out of the temple tipping over the tables of the money changers and driving out the animals and telling the owners of the birds to remove them. This is a good model for proper use of anger because it is effective but not violent. There was no resistance to his actions because all involved knew that what they were doing was wrong. (John 2:13-17.)

In the second instance Jesus again takes issue with an ungodly observance of the Sabbath that prevented healing on this day. He is angry and justly so at their misunderstanding of the purpose of Sabbath worship and the keeping of man-made addendums to the laws. (John 7:21-24)

The largest body of teaching on anger in the New Testament comes from Paul's writings. The following are the points Paul makes.

Paul's principles on anger

1. Never take out vengeance	Romans 12:19
2. Get angry.	Ephesians 4:26
3. In your anger don't sin	Ephesians 4:26
4. Do not stay angry from one day to the next.	Ephesians 4:26
5. Do not let your anger give satan a foothold.	Ephesians 4:27
6. Put away from you all wrath/rage, outcry, blasphemy and malice.	Ephesians 4:31
7. Love each other in a forgiving way just as in Christ God forgave us.	Ephesians 4:32
8. Bear with one another with humility, gentleness and patience, expressing love.	Ephesians 4:2
9. Bear with each other and forgive every complaint even as Christ forgave us.	Colossians 3:13.

Notice that the emphasis on forgiveness, patience, gentleness and love is the opposite of anger and is part of the antidote of dealing with anger.

When we become angry, we are still required to behave in a Christian way and that is with the fruit of the Spirit which is, love, joy, peace, patience, kindness, goodness, faithfulness, gentleness, and self-control. Paul finishes this section with an admonition to not be conceited or to envy or provoke one another. Basically he is saying do not be the cause of other people's anger where possible. (Galatians 5:22-26.)

The book of Hebrews encourages us to not provoke God to anger because it will not go well for us and the writer cites the rebellion of the Israelites in the wilderness who did not achieve their goal of going to the promised land but all died before that happened. (Hebrews 3:9-11.)

The final teaching on anger is in the book of the Revelation. We are told that the nations are angry but their anger is not righteous but is rebellion against God. God is angry with the rebellion of all who have rebelled and history ends with the judgement of all the rebels and rewards for the faithful believers. God justly blames the unrighteous for the destruction of the earth. (Rev 11:18)

CHAPTER 5

I Don't Know Why I Get Angry

Sometimes, people do not know why they are becoming angry. This is usually because they do not understand the process of anger, and this will most likely become apparent when an understanding of the anger cycle is achieved. For people in this category, and for those who have relationships with others who have bouts of anger that seem unaccountable, it is essential the anger cycle is understood. If you cannot work it out yourself, please see a competent counsellor who will be able to explain it to you. I recommend the services of VMTC (Victorious Ministry Through Christ) for committed Christians and any competent counsellor for those who do not have a faith.

There is always a reason for anger, and it is imperative those reasons are known. Otherwise, anger is impossible to remedy. Doping patients with drugs is not a cure, but just a treatment to stabilise the mind. A real cure is possible when we deal with the causes of anger.

Overcoming an Angry Attitude

The following is an outline of how to overcome an angry attitude:

1. Predetermined course of action

If we are prone to becoming angry, the first thing we need to do is to have a predetermined course of action. To have a predetermined course of action, we need to understand the anger triggers which are:

- When someone breaks our **belief** system.
- When someone frustrates our **goal**.
- When someone questions anything we **value**.

2. Change expectations

One of the things we can do is to change our expectations.

- When the problem is with our belief system, we can ask:

  - Is this belief absolutely necessary?
  - Can I expect this belief to be accepted by everyone?
  - Is this belief a universal truth?

- When the problem is with our goals, we can ask:

  - Is this goal realistic?
  - Does my goal impinge on other people's goals?
  - Can I change my goal so that I am satisfied and others are also happy?

- When the problem is with our value, so that people are devaluing us, we need to understand that our value is not set by man or even by ourselves. Our value has been set by God. Because Jesus paid for our sin on the cross, he has given us an eternal value. This value enables us to be classed as God's children and, if we have committed ourselves to Jesus, it classes us as citizens of the kingdom of heaven, entitled to the gift of eternal life. God has such a high value on human beings, he has forbidden anyone to take a human life unless that person has taken another human life. When others place a value on us that is lower than God's value of us, it is a lie. It is not true and is not to be believed and should be disregarded as nonsense.
- When the problem is with the value of an animal or pet, we may need to be patient unless that value is threatening a life (in which case we may have to take some other action).

3. Understand and consider the alternatives

Thirdly, we need to understand and consider the alternatives. Instead of becoming enraged:

- We can choose to be patient with people who cause the incident.
- We can choose to not react to provocation.
- We can choose to be a peacemaker instead of a fighter.
- We can choose to be a responsible communicator instead of a verbal brawler.
- We can choose to adjust our individual belief that is being challenged, unless that belief is truth. Then we can choose to respect the other person and their perspective but not change our belief in truth.
- We can choose to adjust our goal that has been frustrated.
- We can choose to not react to the lie that we are not valuable or that someone else or something else is not valuable. That is, we do not have to respond immediately but can be measured in our response.

4. Do not believe the devil, temptation (sin) is crouching at your door.

Fourthly, we need to not believe the devil who will speak to our mind telling us all kinds of lies that will lead us into sin. Remember, sin is crouching at our door but all we need to do, as A.W. Tozer said, is to talk back to the devil. We should tell him to get lost in the name of Jesus and to get out of our minds. I usually respond by saying something like, "That is not what God says" or "That is not what God wants; go away."

How Should We Respond to Bouts of Anger?

In Chapter 3, I suggested an eight-step method of dealing with anger. This section looks at response from a slightly different perspective.

A. Incident

Every bout of anger begins with an incident where either our **belief** system is broken, our **goals** are frustrated, or a **value** (sometimes ours) is questioned.

B. Anger, without Sin

We then become hurt and become angry, but this should be done without sinning. We are in a very vulnerable place when we have been in a conflict where we have become angry. In this state we are most likely to do or say something that will make matters worse. This is the time to be very careful of our thoughts, speech and actions.

C. Meditate in a Safe Place (e.g. On Our Bed)

Where possible, we should seek to resolve the matter. If this is not possible, we should remove ourselves from the conflict site to a safe place— any other place where we can think things out. Our bed is a good place to do this. If this is not possible, we need to ask, "What happened"? "How did it happen"? "Why did it happen"? "What do I need to do now"? "What should I not do now"?

When for some reason the bedroom is not appropriate like in my situation where my wife was already in the bedroom, another place is necessary like going for a walk. This will also burn off some of the adrenalin that our bodies produce when we become angry.

D. Deal with the Heart (Feelings)

Next, we need to do a self-check of our feelings and emotions. This does not need to be brief. But if we are having this conflict with a close relative or spouse, it would be prudent to tell them we need time out to think things through.

E. Do Not React Quickly (Be Still)

We should not be too hasty and should take all the time we need to understand what is happening.

F. Decide To Resolve the Issues As Much As It Depends upon Us

Work towards resolution as it is the very best solution. We ought to do as much as we can, keeping in mind that others have a right to free choice. A choice made because it was forced upon a person will probably not last.

G. Be Kind

It is very hard to be kind and nasty at the same time; in fact, it is impossible. If our first response is kindness, then an inappropriate response when we get angry is also impossible. Of course, this must be a plan, otherwise other emotions which may be inappropriate will take over. This is something that needs practice to be effective.

H. Be Tenderhearted

Being tenderhearted is also a predetermined response, but it is a Christian response. We need to be looking for the best in people instead of the worst. A soft heart is good preparation for conflict, for conflict will come; and if we are not prepared, the worst may take place.

I. Be Careful Not To Let Sin Occur, Letting The Devil Get A Foothold

Consistent sin opens the door for us to be demonized, but even if we do not become demonized, persistent sinful behavior gives the devil a foothold in our lives. This separates us from God, who is our strength and hope to live peaceful, productive, and victorious lives. For those who do not have a Christian faith or who do not believe in a person becoming demonized it is important to be careful about the thoughts that come into our minds. We will need to examine these thoughts and be aware of the consequences of following these thoughts.

J. Be Careful What We Say. No Corrupt Word

Taking care with the words we use when we are in conflict will reduce the possibility of violence, and it may calm the violent person down. Corrupt words, like swearing or provocative dialogue, may cause the situation to escalate—leading to violence.

K. Explain the Situation Using Positive Dialogue

When necessary, during conflict or even afterwards, we should use positive dialogue, taking responsibility for our part in the conflict. When we make statements like, "You made me angry," we are not speaking the truth because no one can make us angry. Anger may well be our response, but no one forces us to respond that way. Anger is an automatic reaction our bodies make but the way we choose to respond is a choice we make. We may say something like, "I became angry when you said or did something." This accepts the responsibility for our part in becoming angry, whilst factually stating why we made the choice of our response. This is very important because when we say, "You made me angry," we are blaming the other person for a choice we made. Whenever we stray into the area of untruth, we are escalating the possibility of violence. We need to remember that anger is an automatic response of our bodies but the response we make in words or actions is our choice and nobody makes us do it, we choose it.

We need to heed what James said about the tongue in James 3:6-11. The tongue is difficult to tame because it is like a fire and inflames situations. It can be a deadly poison. It is also true that with the tongue we can heal and soothe, we can mediate and help, we can bless and bring joy. Choose our words well and we will avoid difficulties and be an instrument of happiness.

L. Impart Grace to the Hearers

Imparting grace is giving a gift. In the case of conflict, the gift we ought to give is peace. Peace is the opposite of conflict, so it will work towards resolution instead of destruction.

M. Do Not Grieve the Holy Spirit (Check: Attitude, Thoughts, Words, and Heart)

The Holy Spirit is grieved by unholy conduct in word or action. When the Holy Spirit is grieved, so is God the Father and his Son Jesus. We should constantly check our attitudes, thoughts, words, and the purity of our hearts. This will give us harmony. Disharmony is where all our anger problems come from. Harmony begins with us but will spread to other people as we practise it. All people like harmony and are attracted to people who have it and show it.

N. Check for Resentment and Bitterness

When we have resentment and bitterness, we are already on the way to turmoil, so we need to continually ask, "Do I resent anyone or anything? Any race, behavior, mannerism, or anything at all?" If we do, it is sin and needs to be confessed and repented of. Resentment is part of the journey of unforgiveness and bitterness, and it will always end badly for us and for others. This is where we need to nip it in the bud.

O. Forgive (As Christ Forgave Us)

The ultimate way to deal with unforgiveness is to forgive. God promises not only to forgive us but to also cleanse us from all unrighteousness (1 John 1:9).

There is a flow chart of the anger cycle in Appendix 1

CHAPTER 6

Anger and Demonisation

One of the things we need to consider when dealing with anger is demonisation. In my ministry to people with anger problems, I saw many times that people were delivered of a spirit of anger. Although I still believe this is possible, I believe anger or a spirit of anger is sometimes not the problem, as anger is mostly an emotion and not an action. In my own case, the problem was not a spirit of anger but a spirit of rebellion that caused anger outbursts or wrath. In another case, the problem was unforgiveness— and when forgiveness was given, the anger ceased. As I have previously noted, anger is a secondary emotion, so the cause that is driving the anger may be a whole range of conditions (including demonisation) but not necessarily a spirit of anger. In my ministry to people who had anger problems the cure was often dealing with a root of bitterness and when forgiveness was given the anger ceased.

Mark and Luke, in their Gospel accounts, both report an incident where a man—who exhibited remarkable strength powerful enough to break chains and shackles—was demonised. He lived among the tombs and would cry out and gash himself with stones. The demons that were driven out by Jesus were violent and caused 2,000 pigs to rush down a hill and drown in the sea of Galilee. The practice by many people doing deliverance is to name a spirit after the behaviour exhibited by the person with the demon. Jesus did not do that but called the demon an unclean spirit. The spirit calls himself "Legion," explaining they are many, thus, the name Legion.

We need to get to the root of the problem to gain lasting freedom from anger-driven problems. The point I am making is: people who exhibit signs of anger may not be cured by delivering them from a spirit of anger which is the practice by many in ministry. Having said this, demonisation (commonly known as demon possession) is a possibility and needs to be explored.

See Appendix 3 for more discussion about anger and demonisation.

CHAPTER 7

Dave's Story

Dave came to me because he had an anger problem that was causing a problem at work, at home, and with members of his family. I invited Dave (not his real name) to come to dinner with his wife where we discussed his situation. I suggested both Dave and his wife keep an incident diary that recorded events of anger. They were to record what happened, how they responded, and what they could have done differently. They both agreed, so we met at our home for dinner and a chat every two weeks. After dinner, we would open the diaries and discuss the incidents. I would ask them how they could have avoided the situations. We met for several months where we spoke about the issues they were having, and I taught them the information on understanding anger that I have included in this book. I would often ask them what they would do differently in the light of our discussions.

The breakthrough came as we talked one night. It happened when I told them when we are unforgiving, the person or persons whom we do not forgive control our lives. Often the people who have caused our problems sleep well, and they are often unaware of the tension in our relationship. On the other hand, we do not sleep well. We continually go over the issues that have happened, even planning ways that we can get our revenge to cause them to experience the pain we have felt.

Dave responded that this was how he felt, and that he did not want them controlling his life. I told him the moment he forgave them;

he would be free from their control. He went to his dad, telling him of his decision and that he forgave him for specific things that had happened between them. His dad said it did not matter because it was water under the bridge and in the past. Dave said he believed if he forgave everyone who had offended him, he would be free and happy. Although his dad did not agree with him, Dave went ahead with his forgiveness. Dave did the same thing with his sister who responded in the same way as his father had. Dave persisted even though neither he, nor his father or sister, were believers in Christ. Dave followed the same procedure at work and reported that he now felt much better, and that his anger was no longer a problem. To my knowledge, neither Dave nor his wife became believers, but his anger was no longer a problem.

Dave had learned an important lesson: unforgiveness affects us more than the person whom we will not forgive does. It is true that unforgiveness is like drinking poison and expecting the other person to die. Unforgiveness is a poison in our lives that will affect us negatively and may cause health problems that will end our lives prematurely. Although forgiveness is mainly spoken about by Christians, it is not just a Christian thing. It is a universal principle that God has wisely told us to implement in our lives because it really is the only solution to anger-related issues and good relationships. Relationships can never flourish without forgiveness from all participants.

CHAPTER 8

Living with an Angry Person

Veronica E. Coman

Growing up in a peaceful and loving home, I did not experience anger or conflict. As a family we attended church regularly. I believed in God, read the Bible, prayed, and lived what I thought was a 'good' life. However, my belief was just head knowledge. I was quite a reserved person and was happy and content during my school years, nursing training and work and had little conflict. When I married someone who became angry at times, I did not know how to deal with the situation and became increasingly confused and fearful.

Before Patrick and I were married, there was an incident that should have alerted me to the fact that he had a problem with anger. During my midwifery training, I was living in nurses' quarters. Patrick came to see me, but I was out with one of my colleagues. One of my fellow trainees told him this and said I would be back soon. When I returned, we went out, and he kept asking who I had been with. He didn't believe I had been out with a girlfriend but was jealous, and he became very angry when I insisted, I had not been with another man. The angrier he became, the faster he drove, ignoring red lights and stop signs. I was terrified and pleaded with him to slow down, but he did not until we arrived back at the nurses' home.

In a relationship, it can be so easy to justify and repress the feelings of fear we have and continue without dealing with or resolving the issues.

This might seem to be the easiest way to deal with things at the time, but it is very destructive behaviour, long-term, especially in a marriage.

Out of fear, I retreated from the situation and repressed my feelings. I could not, or would not, talk about things. In my mind, I thought this would exacerbate the situation. Because I felt I could not express myself clearly, I clammed up and went into the bedroom and lay crying on my bed. I was too ashamed to talk to anyone about what was happening. Instead, I hid the situation from everyone, including my family.

The fear became deep-seated, and anger developed. My angry responses to Patrick's angry outbursts made matters worse. I became part of the problem.

During one of our arguments, I became so angry that when Patrick threatened to hit me, I stuck out my chin, and said, "Go on then; do it." He punched the refrigerator instead of me. In the morning, when he asked me to take him to hospital, I was still so full of hurt and anger, I told him, "You did it; you fix it." I did not stop to think about how much pain Patrick was in but only that I wanted to hurt him.

Although my behaviour was quite irrational, I did not stop to think about the consequences. Instead of retreating away from the situation or repressing my feelings, like I did in the beginning, I let my anger explode. I spoke out of rage and even hit Patrick. I made choices I knew to be wrong and compromised my belief that I ought not react angrily. Gradually my self-esteem dropped, and I lost confidence in myself. I had become a person I did not like very much.

One evening, on the farm, when Patrick came home for dinner, he became angry over something and threw the plate at the door. I thought I had prepared a nice meal and could not understand why he was angry. This was yet another incident that hurt me.

I repressed the anger for so long, I became resentful and bitter. Residual anger had built up and I exploded, wanting to hurt Patrick. He had hurt me, and I wanted to hurt him. It is so true that 'hurt people hurt people.' That was us. However, later on, we also came to see that 'healed people heal people.'

There were also times I would say what I thought Patrick wanted me to say, to avoid creating conflict. For instance, he would ask, "Do you mind if I go fishing?" I would say, "No, it's OK". Then, I would slam the door, indicating I did mind. I was angry he was going off to enjoy himself while I stayed home doing housework. Instead of communicating what I really felt, I caused a problem.

Patrick mentioned the violent incident after which he dropped me and our girls off at my parents' home. When he asked me to help him with his cleaning job, I considered it was too late for the children to be out. Our eldest was two years old and the other just a baby. I became very angry when he took our eldest daughter out to the car. Not wanting to let her go with Patrick, I decided I also needed to go, so I ran out with the baby in her carry basket.

As Patrick drove, we argued, and I just wanted to get away and take the girls. The car slowed down and, being quite irrational, I got out and started to get the carry basket out. What happened next shocked me: Patrick hit me. After getting back into the car, Patrick drove me to my parents' home and then went off to do the cleaning.

Mum comforted me; however, she also made me face reality. The fault was not all Patrick's. He was very wrong, but it takes two to cause an argument and problems in a marriage. Mum reminded me I married Patrick "for better or for worse." She said, "Go home and the two of you make it work." This was an incredible thing for a mother to do! Many years later I realised she continually prayed for us, and God answered her prayers. By the time Patrick came home, we had both calmed down. We were able talk things through and move on from this crisis. Mum helped to save our marriage.

This situation was my experience and things have turned out well for us. However, this is not the same in other violent relationships. Living with an angry violent person can be very dangerous and even life threatening. There are now many supportive groups to help and guide or even intervene where necessary. We were the fortunate ones who found help through family and our new-found faith in Jesus.

For the first nine years of our marriage, angry outbursts eroded our close relationship. Although there were only a couple of incidents of physical violence, we hurt each other a lot with our words spoken in anger. There were times I just wanted to get away from all the conflict. However, in the end, I was committed to Patrick, our marriage, and our children. I just decided I must continue to try to make our relationship work. Marriage was for life. It was difficult, at times, but we remained committed to each other. Our life was not all bad. We enjoyed many happy, good times; and our love remained even though it was sometimes sorely tested.

On the second of April 1977, everything changed. I asked Jesus to come into my life. God drew me to Himself, and I made my commitment to Him the evening Patrick prayed to receive Jesus. Our life, my life, changed immensely. Now God was present in our lives and marriage. We started to see there was a way through fear, anger, and conflict. Over time, we realised it was possible to talk through differences rationally. We could choose not to let anger rule our lives. There was a new way to live, guided by the Bible.

For example, Proverbs 15:1 says, "A soft answer turns away wrath, but a harsh word stirs up anger." When I responded to Patrick's anger with harsh words, the conflict escalated. When I responded with a soft word, an argument was frequently averted.

Scripture also tells us God has forgiven all our sin and we are to forgive others their sin against us. This was revolutionary for us. We could, and did, forgive one another. This enabled us to continue to improve our relationship

One of the tragic outcomes of our angry outbursts toward each other was that our children were affected. They were still quite young but were hurt and became fearful. I tried to shield and protect them, but we did not "go behind closed doors," and they saw and heard too much. Praise God! He has not only brought change and healing into our lives but also into theirs.

Patrick, in his story, states it took years for his anger problem to be dealt with. Even when we had known the Lord for years, conflict occurred and still needed to be resolved. It took me a long time to stop being fearful of Patrick. It took many years for me to completely trust him. He would still speak angrily but he was no longer violent toward me. It also took many more years for me to completely forgive him for all the hurt and fear his anger caused me. I needed to go to the Lord and confess my angry actions and words and accept that he forgives me.

Patrick has mentioned Victorious Ministry Through Christ. This ministry was the most effective one that brought healing and wholeness into my life. Over years of ministry, I became a more confident person and was able to face difficulties with faith that God was working in me. I also learnt to share problems with Christian friends whom I could trust. They listened, prayed, and walked alongside me. I spent time with the Lord, daily, and he is my great comforter and guide but, at the right time, he had people there for me.

God also used me to come alongside others and minister to them. Many times, he has used me to help, comfort, and bring healing to others who have had similar experiences to mine. God says, "We know that all things work together for good to those who love God, to those who are the called according to His purpose" (Romans 8:28). God does not want us to experience hurt and trauma, but—when we do—he can bring us through to be stronger. He does not want anger to control us and for us to become wrathful, so we hurt others. He brings good out of bad situations, not only for us but for others, too. If we allow God to lead us, he will use us for the good of others.

Proverbs 22:24,25 warns us to "make no friendship with an angry man and with a furious man do not go, lest you learn his ways and set a snare for your soul." Looking back over my relationship with an angry man, I see my soul was snared and I became an angry woman. This was almost a catastrophe for our marriage. If God had not rescued us when he did, our marriage would probably have ended in disaster.

God saved my life and my marriage. He healed my hurts. He gave me peace instead of anger, love instead of fear.

When I look back and remember my past way of life and my responses to anger, I should not live with regrets. I need to let go of the past and learn from my mistakes and the mistakes of others. I need to forgive myself and others. I need to commit to a new way of dealing with anger and live in peace.

I have chosen to be quiet and defuse conflict. I will not allow fear to take hold of me. I have chosen to let Patrick know how I am feeling and talk through the issues. I have chosen to no longer run away and hide but, try to resolve problems. When I feel it is necessary I will leave the situation until I can come back to try to resolve the problem. I will not allow anger to take hold of my life or allow bitterness and residual anger to remain. I have chosen to deal with each situation as it occurs. I will not wait until there are many problems to deal with. I have chosen to be more open to ask for help, especially from those who love and care for me.

Patrick and I have been married for over 55 years, now, and are enjoying a loving, contented relationship. We are by no means perfect, and we still have occasional times of conflict, but these are soon resolved and are never violent. The past is forgiven, and we anticipate spending the remaining years we have together living in peace.

May you, also, find the peace and happiness I have found.

CONCLUSION

"So then, my beloved brethren, let every man be swift to hear, slow to speak, slow to wrath; for the wrath of man does not produce the righteousness of God."
(James 1:19-20)

"He who is slow to wrath has great understanding, but he who is impulsive exalts folly" (Proverbs 14:29).

Regarding anger, God is the perfect model. His anger has an ultimate purpose: peace. When God created mankind, he put them in an idyllic environment (the Garden of Eden) where peace reigned. There was no need for the emotion of anger. Nothing happened that required anger until mankind sinned. Sin messed everything up and changed the environment and the emotions needed to gain peace. Peace is our ultimate goal: peace with God, peace with other people, and peace with our environment.

Our ultimate place of peace is Eden, or its equivalent, which will be when the New Jerusalem descends to the new earth where believers will spend eternity with the Godhead in perfect peace. So, it seems, in the meantime, our goal in life with other humans and God is to pursue peace with all. This means when we choose to become angry, our goal should be peace. To achieve this state of peace, we will need to intentionally choose pathways in our communications that lead to peace.

All fruit of the Spirit is a pathway to peace whilst the fruit of carnality are all pathways to strife. The fruit of the Spirit is: "love, joy, peace, long suffering, (which is patience) kindness, goodness, faithfulness, gentleness, and self-control" (Galatians 5:22–23). The fruit of carnality or 'the works of the flesh' are: "adultery, fornication, uncleanness, lewdness, idolatry, sorcery, hatred, contentions, jealousies, outbursts of wrath, selfish ambitions, dissensions, heresies, envy, murders, drunkenness, revelries, and the like..." (Galatians 5:19–21).

I have shown that anger when it is not dealt with appropriately will lead us to a root of bitterness and residual anger. This is a continual state of simmering rage, a rage detrimental to our health and emotional wellbeing. This condition can be resolved by forgiving those who have contributed to incidents that have led to us becoming angry, and our choice to hold unforgiveness in our hearts. Therefore, it is necessary to be able to identify in our thoughts or behaviours what I have termed the fruit of the root of bitterness, criticism, sarcasm, grudges and judgementalism. A raised voice or shouting can also indicate the presence of a root of bitterness.

I believe that forgiveness is implied in the fruit of the Spirit. Certainly, we know that love forgives all things. Joy forgives, peace forgives, patience forgives, kindness forgives, goodness forgives, faithfulness forgives, gentleness forgives, and self-control forgives. Carnality never forgives; it leads to unfaithfulness, hatred, contentions, jealousy, outbursts of wrath, dissensions, envy and—in extreme cases—murder.

On our journey of life, we cannot avoid anger. We can approach life with a determination of endeavouring to have positive outcomes from the times we become angry. When we encounter situations of anger, we need to be peacemakers. Also, as much as possible, we should not be part of escalating angry situations, but should still be involved in a safe way.

It is clear that anger is an automatic reaction of the body and mind. I have also proposed ways that we can avoid the escalation of anger to a root of bitterness and residual anger. It has taken me many years to travel from anger to peace because I did not understand why I became angry. I did not understand what the anger triggers were so that I could deal with the problems. I did not understand the detrimental effect of a root of bitterness and the dangers of residual anger. My hope is that others will come to an understanding of these principles and apply them to their lives so that their problems of anger can be averted.

REFERENCES

Mills, H. (2005, June 25). *Physiology of anger.* https://www.youthaodtoolbox.org.au/sites/default/files/documents_global/Physiology%20of%Anger.pdf.

New King James Version. (1982). Thomas Nelson, Inc.

Stanley, C. (2014, July 11). Charles Stanley: *The gift of forgiveness.* https://808bo.com/2014/07/11/charles-stanley-the-gift-of-forgiveness/

Walters, R. P. (1981). *Anger: Yours, mine and what to do about it.* Zondervan.

APPENDIX 1

A Flow Chart of The Anger Cycle

Incident
Belief system broken, Goals frustrated, Value questioned.

↓

Hurt

↓

Anger

↓

Unresolved

↓

Resentment

↓

Bitterness

↓

Root of bitterness
Criticism, Sarcasm, Judgemental attitude, Grudges
Raised voices, Yelling, Revenge

↓

Residual anger >>> Ongoing anger problems

↓

Forgiveness

↓

Repentance and confession

↓

Resolution or Release

APPENDIX 2

A Bible Study on Anger Triggers

Read the following passages of Scripture. Then, place an X in the appropriate box or boxes. Use a pencil, so you can change it if you are wrong.

> **Genesis 4:3–10**
>
> "And in the process of time, it came to pass that Cain brought an offering of the fruit of the ground to the LORD. Abel also brought of the firstborn of his flock and of their fat. And the LORD respected Abel and his offering, but he did not respect Cain and his offering. And Cain was very angry, and his countenance fell. So the LORD said to Cain, "Why are you angry? And why has your countenance fallen? "If you do well, will you not be accepted? And if you do not do well, sin lies at the door. And its desire *is* for you, but you should rule over it." Now Cain talked with Abel his brother; and it came to pass, when they were in the field, that Cain rose up against Abel his brother and killed him.
>
> Then the LORD said to Cain, "Where *is* Abel your brother?" He said, "I do not know. Am I my brother's keeper?" And He said, "What have you done? The voice of your brother's blood cries out to Me from the ground."

How did Cain feel?

Did he feel valued?

Did he feel that he had achieved anything?

Was Cain's belief system broken?

Why was Cain angry?

Belief ☐ 1 John 3:12   **Goal** ☐   **Value** ☐

> **Exodus 2:11–12**
>
> "Now it came to pass in those days, when Moses was grown, that he went out to his brethren and looked at their burdens. And he saw an Egyptian beating a Hebrew, one of his brethren. So he looked this way and that way, and when he saw no one, he killed the Egyptian and hid him in the sand."

What caused Moses to kill the Egyptian?

Belief ☐   **Goal** ☐   **Value** ☐

What charge would he have brought against the Egyptian?

> **Exodus 32:7–9,19–20**
>
> "And the Lord said to Moses, "Go, get down! For your people whom you brought out of the land of Egypt have corrupted *themselves*. "They have turned aside quickly out of the way which I commanded them. They have made themselves a molded calf, and worshiped it and sacrificed to it, and said, 'This *is* your god, O Israel, that brought you out of the land of Egypt!'" And the Lord said to Moses, "I have seen this people, and indeed it *is* a stiff-necked people!
>
> So it was, as soon as he came near the camp, that he saw the calf *and* the dancing. So Moses' anger became hot, and he cast the tablets out of his hands and broke them at the foot of the mountain. Then he took the calf which they had made, burned *it* in the fire, and ground *it* to powder; and he scattered *it* on the water and made the children of Israel drink it."

Why was Moses angry?

Why did he break the tablets?

What would be his charge against them?

Belief ☐   **Goal** ☐   **Value** ☐

> **Judges 15:1–5**
>
> After a while, in the time of wheat harvest, it happened that Samson visited his wife with a young goat. And he said, "Let me go in to my wife, into *her* room." But her father would not permit him to go in. Her father said, "I really thought that you thoroughly hated her; therefore, I gave her to your companion. *Is* not her younger sister better than she? Please, take her instead." And Samson said to them, "This time I shall be blameless regarding the Philistines if I harm them!" ⁴Then Samson went and caught three hundred foxes; and he took torches, turned *the* foxes tail to tail, and put a torch between each pair of tails. When he had set the torches on fire, he let the foxes go into the standing grain of the Philistines, and burned up both the shocks and the standing grain, as well as the vineyards *and* olive groves.

What was his intention when he visited?

Why did Sampson get angry?

Did Sampson think that his father-in-law should have given his wife to another?

Did Sampson feel valued?

Belief ☐   **Goal** ☐   **Value** ☐

> **1 Samuel 18:6–9**
>
> Now it had happened as they were coming home, when David was returning from the slaughter of the Philistine, that the women had come out of all the cities of Israel, singing and dancing, to meet King Saul, with tambourines, with joy, and with musical instruments. So the women sang as they danced, and said:
>
> "Saul has slain his thousands, And David his ten thousands."
>
> Then Saul was very angry, and the saying displeased him; and he said, "They have ascribed to David ten thousands, and to me they have ascribed *only* thousands. Now *what* more can he have but the kingdom?" So Saul eyed David from that day forward.

How did Saul feel when he heard the song?

Who did he want to be the hero of the song?

Belief ☐   **Goal** ☐   **Value** ☐

Had David done anything wrong?

> **Jonah 3:10–4:4,9**
>
> Then God saw their works, that they turned from their evil way; and God relented from the disaster that He had said He would bring upon them, and He did not do it.
>
> But it displeased Jonah exceedingly, and he became angry. So he prayed to the LORD, and said, "Ah, LORD, was this not what I said when I was still in my country? Therefore I fled previously to Tarshish; for I know that You *are* a gracious and merciful God, slow to anger and abundant in loving kindness, One who relents from doing harm. "Therefore now, O LORD, please take my life from me, for *it is* better for me to die than to live!" ⁴Then the LORD said, "Is it right for you to be angry?"
>
> Then God said to Jonah, "Is it right for you to be angry about the plant?" And he said, "It is right for me to be angry, even to death!"

What was Jonah's goal in coming to Nineveh?

Why was Jonah angry?

Would Jonah have normally been upset that a plant died?

Belief ☐   **Goal** ☐   **Value** ☐

> **Luke 9:51–54**
>
> Now it came to pass, when the time had come for Him to be received up, that He steadfastly set His face to go to Jerusalem, and sent messengers before His face. And as they went, they entered a village of the Samaritans, to prepare for Him. But they did not receive Him, because His face was set for the journey to Jerusalem. And when His disciples James and John saw this, they said, "Lord, do You want us to command fire to come down from heaven and consume them, just as Elijah did?"

What specific sin was it that the sons of thunder wished to punish?

Belief ☐   **Goal** ☐   **Value** ☐

> **Acts 9:1–2**
>
> Then Saul, still breathing threats and murder against the disciples of the Lord, went to the high priest and asked letters from him to the synagogues of Damascus, so that if he found any who were of the Way, whether men or women, he might bring them bound to Jerusalem.

Why was Saul angry enough to kill and persecute the Christians?

Belief ☐   **Goal** ☐   **Value** ☐

> The older brother in the Prodigal Son Parable.
>
> **Luke 15:25–30**
>
> "Now his older son was in the field. And as he came and drew near to the house, he heard music and dancing. 'So he called one of the servants and asked what these things meant. 'And he said to him, 'Your brother has come, and because he has received him safe and sound, your father has killed the fatted calf.' 'But **he was angry** and would not go in. Therefore, his father came out and pleaded with him. 'So he answered and said to *his* father, 'Lo, these many years I have been serving you; I never transgressed your commandment at any time; and yet you never gave me a young goat, that I might make merry with my friends. 'But as soon as this son of yours came, who has devoured your livelihood with harlots, you killed the fatted calf for him.'"

Why was the older brother angry?

Belief ☐   **Goal** ☐   **Value** ☐

APPENDIX 3

More Information on Demonisation

Demon possession is a bad term as the person has the demon, not the other way around. The terms used in the original language in the Bible are words like, "he has a demon," "he had the spirit of an unclean demon;" but the term 'possession' is never used.

Jesus used different ways to deliver people from demons. Consider the bold highlighted words in the following passages.

A man with an unclean spirit.

Mark 1:23–26. Jesus rebuked him, saying, **"Be quiet, and come out of him!"** And when the unclean spirit had convulsed him and cried out with a loud voice, he came out of him.

The Gadarene Demoniac.

Mark 5:1–13. Jesus said, **"Come out of the man, unclean spirit!" "What is your name?"** then he gave the demons permission to go into the pigs that rushed down the hill into the water and were drowned.

Luke 8:24–33. Jesus had commanded the unclean spirit to come out of the man.

The Syro-Phoenician woman's daughter

Mark 7:26–30. Jesus said to her, **"For this saying go your way; the demon has gone out of your daughter."**

The man whose son had a mute spirit.

Mark 9:17–29. **"Deaf and dumb spirit, I command you, come out of him and enter him no more!"**

The man whose son was an epileptic.

Matthew 17:14–21. **Jesus rebuked the demon**, and it came out of him; and the child was cured from that very hour.

A man with a spirit of an unclean demon.

Luke 4:33–35. Jesus rebuked him, saying, **"Be quiet, and come out of him!"**

A child with a spirit who seizes him and convulses him.

Luke 9:38–42. **Jesus rebuked the unclean spirit**, and healed the child.

A woman who had a spirit of infirmity.

Luke 13:11–13. **"Woman, you are loosed from your infirmity."** And He laid His hands on her, and immediately she was made straight, and glorified God.

A girl with a python spirit. The original language says python spirit.

Acts 16:16–18. **"I command you in the name of Jesus Christ to come out of her."**

This short study on the practices of Jesus and Paul, doing deliverance, reveals a very simple method. It mostly does not include the use of a name for demons but simply calls them "unclean spirits," followed by the command "Come out!" or—in Paul's case—"I command you in the name of Jesus Christ to come out of her." This seems to be a better version than the one I have often heard in deliverance ministry. Paul is careful to say, "I command you in the name of Jesus," and not, "I command you" which was common in the many sessions of deliverance at which I was present.

Becoming Reinhabited by a Demon

"When an unclean spirit goes out of a man, he goes through dry places, seeking rest; and finding none, he says, 'I will return to my house from which I came.' And when he comes, he finds it swept and put in order. Then he goes and takes with him seven other spirits more wicked than himself, and they enter and dwell there; and the last state of that man is worse than the first" (Luke 11:24–26).

This passage is recorded by both Matthew and Luke and shows that getting rid of the demon or demons can be followed by a reinfestation. Luke begins Chapter 11 with the Lord's prayer and follows it with a lesson on persistence— that is: keep asking, keep seeking, and keep knocking. With these phrases, he emphasises the goodness of God and his desire to give us good gifts, particularly the Holy Spirit. He says we need to ask for, seek for, and persist to have his Spirit in our lives.

He follows this with teaching on deliverance and the nature of demons. Deliverance, to be effective, needs to be done by the finger of God and this probably refers to doing it in the name of Jesus, as Paul did. Luke further points out the need for a strong man to protect us. There is no one stronger than Jesus, for he is God, and his replacement here on earth is the Holy Spirit.

Jesus said that whatever we ask in his name, he will do. He also said that the Father will give us another helper who will dwell with us and will be in us (John 14:16). The Holy Spirit is the power of God in us: not a power we can use for whatever we want, but a power we can use through the name of Jesus for his purposes. As Paul says, "we are his workmanship created in Christ Jesus for good works which God prepared beforehand that we should walk in them" (Ephesians 2:10).

This power to do deliverance is from Jesus, through the Holy Spirit, to do the will of God so that we can also do the will of God. This ministry is to the glory of God and not to our glory as his servant -children. To prevent reinfestation, or to prevent being demonised again, we need to be full of the Holy Spirit. This is what Paul is getting at in Ephesians 5:18 when he says to go on be being filled with the Holy Spirit. The other thing is to remain spiritually clean, so that demons or the devil will not gain a foothold. This is what Paul is saying in Ephesians 4:26–27 "Be angry, and do not sin: Do not let the sun go down on your wrath, nor give place to the devil."

James and Peter have the same thoughts in the following verses. "Therefore, submit to God. Resist the devil and he will flee from you. Draw near to God and He will draw near to you. Cleanse your hands, you sinners; and purify your hearts, you double-minded. Lament and mourn and weep! Let your laughter be turned to mourning and your joy to gloom. Humble yourselves in the sight of the Lord, and He will lift you up" (James 4:7–10). "Be sober, be vigilant; because your adversary the devil walks about like a roaring lion, seeking whom he may devour. Resist him, steadfast in the faith, knowing that the same sufferings are experienced by your brotherhood in the world" (1 Peter 5:8–9).

Demonisation is a real possibility as we struggle to overcome sin in our lives. The clear inference from these verses is that the habitual presence of sin in our lives opens us up to being demonised, particularly in the area of rage. I believe giving a place to the devil in our lives is exactly that, becoming demonised by our consistent involvement in sinful activities. It is clear we will sin, but that is where confession comes in as per 1 John 1:9: "When we confess our sin God is faithful to forgive us our sin and cleanse us of all unrighteousness." There appears to be a culture in modern Christianity of seeing how close we can get to sin without being tainted, instead of a culture of staying so far away from sin we will not become involved with it. We are to be single minded when it comes to sin and not double minded.

If we find ourselves in a situation where we are struggling with giving up a sinful habit, it may be we are demonised. This is nothing to be afraid of as Jesus treats demonisation like an illness and calls 'deliverance from demons' as being healed. There are many different ministries around that do deliverance healing, but not all of them are competent. I have been involved with VMTC (Victorious Ministry Through Christ). This is how I was able to be healed of being demonised, and overcoming my problem with anger or more correctly with rage. They also helped me learn about this important aspect of my Christian walk. I was also able to get six-monthly spiritual check-ups through this ministry which has been a great help. VMTC is in most states of Australia and is also in many other countries.

How To Discern a Spirit

How to discern whether a spirit is of God or is an evil spirit is spoken about by John in 1 John 4:1–6.

The pertinent section is verse 4 that tells us we have overcome evil spirits. Verses 2 and 3 give us a formula we can use. Every spirit that confesses Jesus has come in the flesh is of God, and every spirit that does not confess Jesus Christ has come in the flesh is not of God. This is a good start, but spirits lie; so we must be careful in our assessment. As I was praying about this, after I was challenged by a brother as to whether I really did hear from God, I developed a system to test the voices I heard in my head. Let me digress a little.

When I was in Bible college, I heard a lecture by Dr John Dahms on "How God communicates." He asked us how God communicated to us, and several ways were given. The Bible was the main source followed by sermons, through the creation, through his Holy Spirit, and through other believers. When the lecturer asked if there were any other ways, I offered the opinion that God used spiritual telepathy. There was an uproar from some of the students who thought that telepathy was occult, so God would not use that method. Dr Dahms was thoughtful and stretched his braces like he did when he was thinking and said

"Yes, will you please explain?" I replied that I never hear an audible voice from God, but I have had a thought in my mind that I know is not from my own thoughts. These thoughts can be either the devil, a demon, or God. The lecturer agreed: but how to tell the difference between the voices? I was thinking about this lecture (and question) when I had these thoughts of a system that I began to try, one which has never led me astray.

When I hear a voice, I ask the question based on 1 John 4:2–3.

Was Jesus the Christ born of the virgin Mary and became a human being?

I wait for an answer. If there is no answer, I do not trust the voice. If the voice says "No," I do not trust the voice. But if the answer is "Yes," I ask another question.

"Did Jesus the Christ die for the sins of the world?"

I wait for an answer. If there is no answer, I do not trust the voice. If the voice says "No," I do not trust the voice. But if the answer is "Yes," I ask another question.

"Did Jesus the Christ rise from the dead on the third day and overcome sin death and the devil?"

I wait for an answer. If there is no answer, I do not trust the voice. If the voice says "No," I do not trust the voice. But if the answer is "Yes," I ask another question.

"Did Jesus the Christ ascend into heaven and sit at the right hand of God where he intercedes for us?" I wait for an answer. If there is no answer, I do not trust the voice. If the voice says "No," I do not trust the voice. But if the answer is "Yes," I ask another question. The final question is:

"Is Jesus the Christ coming back to take us to be with him forever?"
I wait for an answer. If there is no answer, I do not trust the voice. If the voice says "No," I do not trust the voice. But if the answer is "Yes," I trust the voice implicitly.

These voices aren't actually voices but are more like thoughts. They can be quite alarming at times and, if we own these thoughts as our own, we can very soon end up under a great weight of sin. This problem of sinful thoughts is easily overcome.

W. Tozer has written a book called *I Talk Back to the Devil*. This book is very helpful. Prayer that is audible is the most effective prayer and speaking audibly back to the devil when we have these sinful or unhelpful thoughts is most effective. When I have these thoughts enter my mind, I am careful not to dwell upon them. I reject them promptly by saying aloud something like, "God does not want me to think those thoughts, so you can just go away," "I reject these thoughts in Jesus' name," or "God doesn't want me to do that; I reject that in Jesus' name." This is important when we are controlling anger in the form of rage. The devil will take advantage of our anger and try to get us to sin, and the Lord has told us to get angry but not to sin.

APPENDIX 4

Scriptures Used in This Book

Old Testament		New Testament	
Gen. 4:3–10	Prov. 15:18	Mt 5:22	Acts 16:16–18
		Mt. 6:15	Rom. 8:28
Ex. 2:11–12	Prov. 16:32	Mt. 17:14–21	Rom 12:19
Ex. 32:7–9, 19–20	Prov. 19:11	Mt. 23:27–33	1Cor. 6:20
Judg. 15:1–5	Prov. 19:19	Mk. 1:23–26	Gal. 5:19–26
1 Sam. 16:14–31:13	Prov. 21:19	Mk. 3:4–5	Eph. 2:10
1 Sam. 18:6–9	Prov. 22:3	Mk. 5:1–13	Eph. 4:2,26–27, 29–32
Ps. 4:4	Prov. 22:24–25	Mk. 7:26–30	Eph. 5:18
Ps. 55:22	Prov. 29:8, 22	Mk. 9:17–29	Phil. 3:12
Prov. 13:3	Eccl. 7:9	Lk. 4:33-35	Col. 2:13-14
Prov. 14:29	Jon. 3:10–4:4, 9	Lk. 8:26–33	Col. 3:6–8,13
Prov. 15:1	Mic. 7:19	Lk. 9:38–42, 51–54	Heb 3:9-14
		Lk. 11:24–26	Heb. 8:12
		Lk. 13:11–13	Heb. 12:14–15
		Lk 14:16-24	Jas. 1:19–20
		Lk. 15:25–32	Jas. 3:6-11
		Jn. 17:11	Jas. 4:7–10
		Jn. 2:13–17	1 Pet. 5:8–9
		Jn 7:21-24	1 Jn. 1:9
		Jn. 14:16	1 Jn. 3:12
		Jn. 17:11	1 Jn. 4:1–6
		Acts 9:1–2	Rev. 11:18

APPENDIX 5

Receiving the Gift of Eternal Life

On my life journey, the greatest help I have had is when—on the second of April 1977—I asked Jesus into my life. From that point on, my life began to change and my lifelong problems with anger began to be dealt with. I have written this book so that others who struggle with anger can also be helped. It is my desire that those who suffer from anger may find peace. It is also my desire that those who live with someone with an anger problem may understand what is happening and be helped.

In my life as a pastor, I was able to help many people with anger problems; and my prayer is that many others will be able to help people in crisis using my material. The very best place to start is to have a relationship with God through Jesus.

My journey from anger to peace began when my pastor asked me if I would like the gift of eternal life.

> Would you like the gift of eternal life?
> Did you know eternal life is free?

We can't buy it or earn it, and we don't deserve it. None of us is perfect for we have all done wrong, thought wrong, or not done what we ought to have done. God calls this sin, so we need help.

Jesus paid for our wrongdoings with his death on the cross.
Jesus paid the penalty for us, so we could be forgiven.
Jesus rose from the grave and conquered death.
Jesus opened the door to eternal life for us.
We can receive the benefits Jesus died for by
accepting what he did and by putting our trust in him.
Believe in your heart that Jesus died for you.
Trust Jesus to give you eternal life.
Accept Jesus into your life.
Tell others what you have done.

You could pray a prayer like this:

Heavenly Father, I have done wrong.
I am sorry.
Jesus, come into my life. I accept you.
I believe you died for me.
I trust you to give me eternal life.
Lord, I really want this to happen.
I ask this in Jesus' name.
Thank you Holy Spirit for guiding me into all truth,
Thank you, Lord Jesus, for coming into my life,
for forgiving my sin, and for cleansing me
from all unrighteousness. Amen.

www.ingramcontent.com/pod-product-compliance
Lightning Source LLC
La Vergne TN
LVHW011722060526
838200LV00051B/2994